XI'AN

Text and Photographs by Simon Holledge

China Guides Series Limited

China Guides Series Limited
Published 1984

Introduction by David Bonavia © China Guides Series Limited 1984
Maps and photographs © Simon Holledge 1984 (represented by
Pacific Press Service, Tokyo and Osaka, Vision International,
London and The Stock Market, New York)
Other photographs on pages 5, 16, 64 and 69 © Jacky Yip 1984
Photograph on page 40 © Sanjo Munetomo 1984
Map artwork by Herman Yiu

China Guides Series Limited
Causeway Bay PO Box 31395
Hong Kong

Printed in Hong Kong by South China Printing Co.

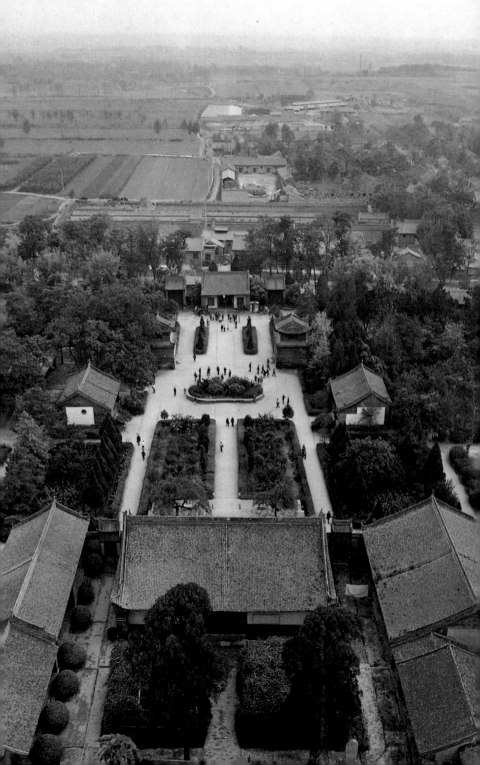

Contents

Maps and Diagrams

The addresses in this book are given in **pinyin** *which is the official romanization system of the Chinese government.* **Dajie** *is a main thoroughfare;* **lu** *and* **jie** *are smaller streets;* **hutong** *and* **xiang** *are lanes or alleys.*

A Brief Chronology of China

Palaeolithic	c.600,000 — 7000 BC
Neolithic	c.7000 — 1600 BC
Shang	c.1600 — 1027 BC
Western Zhou	1027 — 771 BC
Eastern Zhou	770 — 256 BC
Spring and Autumn Annals	770 — 476 BC
Warring States	475 — 221 BC
Qin	221 — 207 BC
Western (Former) Han	206 BC — 8 AD
Xin	9 — 24
Eastern (Later) Han	25 — 220
Three Kingdoms	220 — 265
Western Jin	265 — 316
Northern and Southern Dynasties	317 — 589
Sixteen Kingdoms	317 — 439
• Former Zhao	304 — 329
• Former Qin	351 — 383
• Later Qin	384 — 417
Northern Wei	386 — 534
Western Wei	535 — 556
Northern Zhou	557 — 581
Sui	581 — 618
Tang	618 — 907
Five Dynasties	907 — 960
Northern Song	960 — 1127
Southern Song	1127 — 1279
Jin (Jurchen)	1115 — 1234
Yuan (Mongol)	1279 — 1368
Ming	1368 — 1644
Qing (Manchu)	1644 — 1911
Republic	1911 — 1949
People's Republic	1949 —

An Introduction to Xi'an

By David Bonavia

The city of Xi'an has at different times been the capital of China for longer than any other – a total of some 1100 years.

The magnificent archaeological and art discoveries in and around the city tell the tale of China's development from prehistoric times till the height of the imperial period.

There have been so many amazing finds in the area that only a small proportion of them are as yet on view to the public and tourists. However, a growing number are being put on display.

Xi'an was at different times the capital of the Zhou, Han, Sui and Tang Dynasties. Lying on the Wei River in Shaanxi Province, it commanded the approaches to Central China from the mountains of the northwest. It was also the starting point of the Silk Road of ancient times, which brought Chinese merchandise as far west as the Mediterranean.

The modern city is plain and businesslike, but the narrow residential alleys and street markets bear the flavour of old China. Sections of the old city wall testify to Xi'an's strategic importance down the ages. From there one may visit Yan'an, where the late Chairman Mao Zedong's followers in the Communist Party built up their strength for the final confrontation with Generalissimo Chiang Kai-shek's Nationalist forces. Chiang was actually captured in his nightgown trying to escape from a hot springs resort near Xi'an, by a younger commander who wanted him to unite with the Communists and fight the Japanese – the famous Xi'an Incident of 1936.

Dubbed 'the land of kings and emperors' by Du Fu, China's most famous poet, Xi'an dates back in its origins to the eleventh century BC, when the rulers of the Zhou Dynasty set up Fenghao, a twin city made up of Fengjing and Haojing, about ten miles southwest of the present site. The city was grid-shaped – a pattern which later became common in Chinese cities – and nine carts could ride abreast on each of the eighteen main roads of the grid, it was said.

In the eighth century BC, the Zhou Dynasty moved its capital downstream to Luoyang. A ruler of the Kingdom of Qin, in northwest China, established his capital at Xianyang, just to the north of Xi'an. In 221 BC the King of Qin conquered the other feudal kingdoms to become the first Emperor. Qin Shihuangdi, as he became known, imposed a form of early totalitarianism on China. He consolidated and extended the various sections of the Great Wall which was meant to keep out fierce northern tribesmen. He standardized the Chinese written language and even the span of cart-axles. But his oppressive rule broke down when his son succeeded to the throne, and after a sanguinary civil war a rebel commander called Liu Bang established the Han Dynasty with its capital at the city, which was now called Chang'an.

The Han Dynasty was a period of great cultural flowering and imperial expansion. Pottery, bronze and iron work, lacquer, precious metals, wall-painting and sculpture of a very high artistic standard survive in impressive quantities. One such is the gilt-bronze horse unearthed recently, which has been put on show at the Shaanxi Museum. The city was three times the size of Rome at the time. Chinese and Roman soldiers may actually have crossed swords in Central Asia, but this has not been proven.

Qin Shihuangdi died in 210 BC. In accordance with the custom of the time, it is believed, he had his ministers, family members, slaves and horses buried with him – but whether all of them were actually killed, as would have been normal a few centuries earlier, or whether some were buried later as they naturally died, is not clear. The main part of the tomb remains to be excavated.

But the pottery figures of soldiers and horses leave no doubt that the emperor wanted a bodyguard in the afterlife. There are estimated to be fully 8000 clay warriors, whose existence was discovered by some peasants digging a well in 1974. Each human figure is different from the other – or so it seems – and they are slightly larger than life-size. They wear a variety of uniforms and body-armour, though all have a flowing, knee-length robe, a turned-round lapel, and breeches. They wear their hair in elaborate topknots and sport moustaches. Some are kneeling in postures which suggest that they once held drawn bows of wood, now decayed. The whole tomb area covers nearly 22 square miles. There is an outer wall with four gates, and an inner wall with five – two of them being on the north side. The figures are a fascinating direct link with the past over a period of 22 centuries.

In 25 AD the Eastern Han Dynasty removed the capital to Luoyang. From the third century AD there ensued a period of civil war and division of China into separate kingdoms, sometimes with rival claimants to the title of Emperor. But in 582 the founder of the Sui Dynasty, Yang Jian, restored the city as the capital. It was enlarged and improved, and a famous Chinese poet wrote of it: 'Ten thousand houses look like a laid-out chessboard'. Merchants and tribute bearers from Central and Western Asia arrived there with exotic products. But the new capital shortly fell to Li Yuan, who established the Tang Dynasty. The most famous imperial concubine in Chinese history, the beauty Yang Guifei, and the most powerful Empress, Wu Zetian, inhabited the imperial palace in the Tang Dynasty. In its cultural achievements, the Tang outdid even the Han Dynasty, especially in poetry, painting, music, ceramics and calligraphy.

With the fall of the Tang Dynasty in 907, the capital was removed — after a period of civil war – to the city of Kaifeng in Henan Province in 960 AD, and later, when the Jin Tartars invaded north China, to Hangzhou

達摩出祖元像信

手拈來非上非紙

非墨非我逸人墨

面傳之

己巳仲冬風於寫

in the east. In 1295 the Mongols led by Khubilai Khan conquered all China and established their capital at Peking. The Ming Dynasty (1368 — 1644), while governing from Peking, rebuilt the inner section of the city now called Xi'an, but it was never to be the capital again.

The main tourist attractions are the Ming Dynasty Drum Tower and Bell Tower near the city centre, the Shaanxi Museum, the Big Goose and Little Goose Pagodas, the Great Mosque, surviving portions of the old city wall, the stone-age site at Banpo — and above all the pottery figures buried in the ground to 'guard' Qin Shihuangdi's tomb.

Numerous other imperial tombs are known to exist, though they may have been despoiled by tomb-robbers and will take time to excavate.

Though the city is quite heavily industrialized, the Chinese Government has decided to give priority to excavation and restoration of ancient sites and buildings. Unfortunately much damage has already been done to the old city, which cannot be restored. But when a construction firm recently demolished part of the city wall in contravention of a ban on such vandalism, the authorities ordered the offenders to rebuild it, and made it an exemplary case.

David Bonavia is the China correspondent of **The Times** *of London and of the Hong Kong-based* **Far Eastern Economic Review.**

Getting to Xi'an

Before the Second World War the few foreigners who made the arduous journey to Xi'an considered themselves adventurers rather than tourists. To reach their destination they had to travel to the end of the railway line in the neighbouring province of Henan, and then transfer to bumpy carts for a further journey of six days through 'bandit infested' country. The journey became easier when the railway reached Xi'an in 1934. A palatial station was erected, which is still in use today. The opulent waiting rooms are worth looking at if you are at the station. Today Xi'an has become the main communications centre for the northwest region of China.

By air There are still no international flights to Xi'an, though the Chinese airline, CAAC (Civil Aviation Administration of China), ran some chartered flights direct from Hong Kong during 1983.

At present independent travellers come through Hong Kong, via Guangzhou (Canton), or through Tokyo, via Shanghai. Tokyo to Xi'an via Beijing takes slightly longer than via Shanghai, and costs more. Connections between Hong Kong and Guangzhou, Tokyo and Shanghai, and Tokyo and Beijing, are frequent. But CAAC have only three Guangzhou – Xi'an flights a week, taking about 4 hours, and these should be booked well in advance. From Shanghai there are five flights a week taking 2¾ hours, and from Beijing 14 flights, lasting 2 hours. There are also air connections with Changsha, Chengdu, Chongqing, Kunming, Lanzhou, Nanjing, Taiyuan and Zhengzhou. Xi'an airport does not have radar and planes are occasionally delayed for long periods, waiting for clear weather.

By rail Xi'an is on the Longhai Line, the main east–west railway starting at Lianyungang, a port facing the Yellow Sea, and ending in the Xinjiang Uygur Autonomous Region, Chinese Central Asia. Express trains arrive daily from Beijing (taking about 21 hours) and also from Shanghai, Nanjing, Qingdao, Zhengzhou, Wuchang, Chongqing, Chengdu, Lanzhou, Ürümqi and Taiyuan. Luoyang, the historic 'Eastern Capital', is 240 miles (387 km) to the east of Xi'an. The journey takes 7 hours and there are trains every day.

Climate and Clothing

Xi'an's climate is much drier and cooler than that of southwest or southeast China, and less extreme than that of Beijing. In American terms the climate is analogous to that of Wyoming. The Qinling Mountains to the south of the Wei River Valley shield Xi'an from the southeastern monsoon, which brings much rain and considerable humidity to the neighbouring province of Sichuan. Annual precipitation is only 21 to 24 inches (530 –600 mm). Most of the rainfall occurs in July, August and September.

Vistors arrive in large numbers from March onwards: many residents believe that spring is the best season, with the city at its most beautiful under clear, bright skies. Summer begins in May, usually fine and sunny. The hottest month is July when noon temperatures may reach 100°F (38°C). Late summer and early autumn is cooler and can be overcast. Late autumn is usually fine and winter is dry with a little snow. At night during winter temperatures may drop below 0°F (– 17°C).

Xi'an has not been a city of official pomp for a long time now and formal attire is not required. In mid-summer only the lightest clothing is necessary, in mid-winter thermal underwear and multi-layered clothing add to comfort.

Mean Temperatures for Xi'an

	F°	C°		F°	C°		F°	C°
January	27	– 3	May	68	20	September	68	20
February	36	2	June	79	26	October	55	13
March	46	8	July	81	27	November	45	7
April	57	14	August	79	26	December	34	1

Hotels

Xi'an did not have a western-style hotel until the 1950s. In the early part of the century Chinese inns were open to foreigners, but many western travellers arriving in Xi'an stayed with the European missionaries of the Scandinavian Alliance, the English Baptist Mission and the China Inland Mission.

Xi'an has been one of China's biggest tourist bottlenecks since the rapid expansion of the tourist industry in 1978. Despite the recent opening of several large new tourist hotels, there is still likely to be an accommodation shortage during peak months.

Hotels in Xi'an, as elsewhere in China, offer a confusing array of room classes and prices. Accommodation ranges from vast old-fashioned suites to dingy dormitories. Foreign travellers, foreign experts or students resident in China, and Chinese, each pay a different price for the same room. Tourists travelling in a group will be allocated a hotel by CITS (China International Travel Service), and visitors travelling independently should not necessarily expect a free choice of accommodation.

人民大厦　东新街
People's Mansion (Renmin Dasha) Dongxin Jie tel. 25111
This hotel, with its Soviet-style facade behind yellow, red and black painted iron railings, was occupied by Russian technical personnel in the 1950s, but was built by the Chinese. The 195-room front building was completed in 1953, the back building, with 153 rooms, in 1957.

All rooms are airconditioned and heated, and most have telephones. There are four dining rooms, the main one being in a separate building to the east of the front building. There is a coffee shop and bar (open 8pm — 11 pm) in a screened-off section of the main dining room, and there is another bar on the third floor of the front building. Other facilities include a bank, telecommunications desk, two souvenir shops, and a games room.

Situated in the northeastern section of the walled city, the People's Mansion is within walking distance of Revolution Park to the north, and the shopping district of Nanxin Jie and Dong Dajie (East Avenue) to the south.

西安宾馆　长安路
Xi'an Guesthouse Chang'an Lu tel. 51351
Designed to take the pressure off the People's Mansion, this high-rise hotel opened at the end of 1981. The white 13-storey building is a prominent landmark. The hotel provides full services, including bars on the first and second floors that sell French, Italian and German wines for 6 or 8 *yuan* a glass accompanied by Cantonese and Japanese pop music. It commands a good view due north to the South Gate and beyond to the Bell Tower, and

also southeast to the Big Goose Pagoda. It is separated by a few fields from the Little Goose Pagoda. This well-run hotel is becoming a favourite with foreign visitors.

钟楼饭店
Bell Tower Hotel (Zhonglou Fandian) tel: 22033/24730
This ideally located hotel was opened in January 1983. There are 300 rooms on seven floors overlooking the Bell Tower and busy streets that form the Bell Tower circle. Although designed and built by the Chinese in some haste, its size, location and convenience make it the third most important hotel in the city.

陕西宾馆 丈八沟
Shaanxi Guesthouse Zhangbagou tel. 23831
Formerly for the exclusive use of high-ranking officials, foreign VIPs and diplomats, this expensive guesthouse was opened to tourists in 1977. It is set in beautiful secluded gardens with a lake, close to the River Bi, about 10½ miles (17 km) southwest of the city centre. The guesthouse complex consists of 10 two-storey residential buildings, constructed in the 1950s. There are 178 guest rooms and eight separate restaurants. Some of the suites are prodigiously large by international standards and can cost up to 500 *yuan* a night.

华清池宾馆 临潼县
Huaqing Guesthouse Lintong County
Although this small 30-bed hotel is 19 miles (30 km) outside Xi'an, it has a particularly attractive location. It occupies the southwest corner of the Huaqing Palace Hotsprings, not far from the Mausoleum of the First Emperor of Qin and the Qin Terracotta Army Museum. The single-storey buildings are in Tang architectural style and hot spa water is piped into all the bathrooms.

There are several other hotels in Xi'an that travellers on a low budget might try. The cheap **Victory Hotel,** south of Heping Gate and close to the Provincial Song and Dance Theatre, is used mainly by Overseas Chinese and local people. **Jiefang Hotel,** across the square from the train station on the left, is a friendly but dingy hotel only recommended to those who want to keep accommodation costs to a minimum. **Xi'an Restaurant** at the intersection of Dong Dajie (East Avenue) and Juhuayuan (tel. 22127) may also have some rooms available.

Modern Xi'an

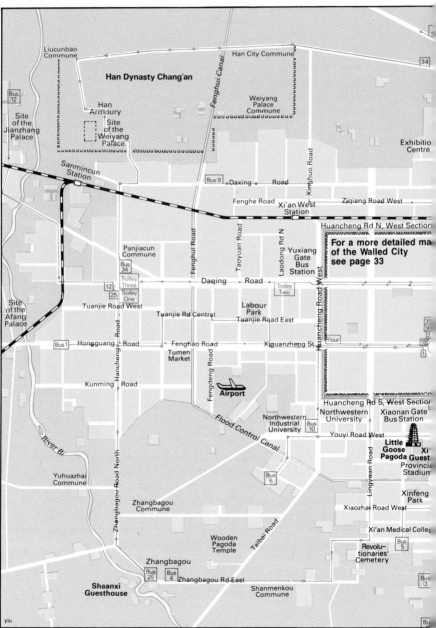

Liucunbao Commune

Han City Commune

34

Han Dynasty Chang'an

Bus 12

Fenghui Canal

Weiyang Palace Commune

Site of the Jianzhang Palace

Han Armoury

Site of the Weiyang Palace

Exhibition Centre

Sanmincun Station

Xinghuo Road

Bus 9 Daxing Road

Fenghe Road   Xi'an West Station   Ziqiang Road West

Huancheng Rd N, West Section

For a more detailed map of the Walled City see page 33

Panjiacun Commune

Fenghui Road

Taoyuan Road

Laodong Rd N

Yuxiang Gate Bus Station

Bus 34

12 25

Trolley Three

Trolley One

Daqing Road

Trolley Two

Huancheng Road West

Site of the Afang Palace

Tuanjie Road West

Tuanjie Rd Central

Labour Park

Tuanjie Road East

Four

35
36

18

Bus 1 Hongguang Road

Hancheng Road

Fenghao Road

Tumen Market

Fengdeng Road

Xiguanzheng St

1

Kunming Road

Airport

Flood Control Canal

Zhangbagou Road North

River Bi

Northwestern Industrial University

Bus 10

Northwestern University

Xiaonan Gate Bus Station

Huancheng Rd S, West Section

Youyi Road West

Lingyuan Road

Little Goose Pagoda Guest

Xi'

Provincial Stadium

Yuhuazhai Commune

Bus 6

Xinfeng Park

Zhangbagou Commune

Xiaozhai Road West

Taibai Road

Xi'an Medical College

Wooden Pagoda Temple

Revolu- tionaries' Cemetery

Bus 5

Bus 3

Zhangbagou

Shaanxi Guesthouse

Bus 25

Bus 4 Zhangbagou Rd East

Shanmenkou Commune

yiu

Bu

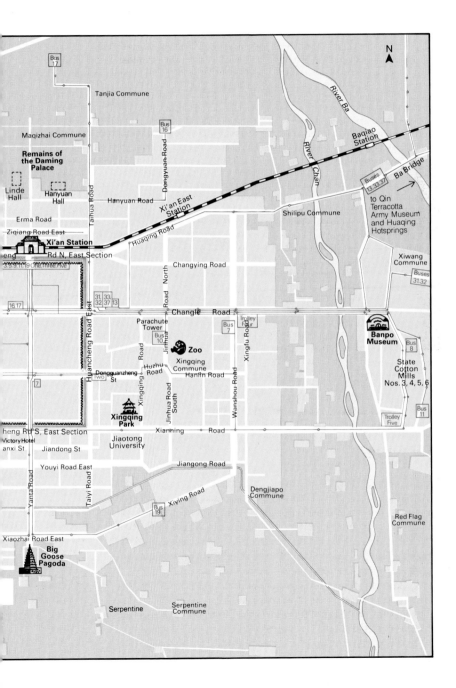

Getting around Xi'an

Some areas within the city walls are well worth exploring on foot. The streets around the Drum Tower and the Great Mosque have a particularly high concentration of interesting old buildings. The area around the Bell Tower and the busy shopping streets of Dong Dajie (East Avenue) and Xi Dajie (West Avenue) are also worth looking at on foot. You may stumble across other old neighbourhoods if you walk in the areas round the North and East Gates, and in the streets north and west of the Shaanxi Museum.

There are five trolleybus lines in the city and a number of bus lines, some of which extend into the newly developed urban areas (see map on pages 20 and 21). Public transport is cheap but impractical unless you have full directions already written out in Chinese, or a basic knowledge of the language. Taxis are available at the hotels, but cannot be hailed in the streets. They charge by kilometre travelled. Taxi drivers rarely speak English so get your instructions written out in Chinese before you set out.

Many of the more important places of interest are a long way from the city. Tour groups will be taken out in comfortable Japanese-made buses owned by CITS. Independent travellers could take a taxi, and possibly hire a guide-interpreter from CITS. Less expensive would be a day-tour on an airconditioned bus (6 yuan in 1983 including pickup at your hotel) which takes in the Qin Tomb and Terracotta Army, Banpo and Huaqing Hotsprings. To book a seat walk east from the Bell Tower and take the first right. The tour office is about 100 yards down on the left. A similar tour can be booked from another company whose booking office is at Jiefang Hotel. There is also a booking office at the Bell Tower Hotel. The addresses and telephone numbers of various long distance and outer district public bus stations are given on page 93.

Shopping

Earlier this century Xi'an was known for its curio shops stocked with antiquities of the city. Today, however, visitors should not expect to find anything particularly old; objects for sale date from the Qing and Republic periods. Xi'an's principal antique shop, the **Xi'an City Antique Store**, is handsomely housed inside the Drum Tower. Stock is varied and attributions are reliable, but there is nothing special that cannot be found in similar stores in other Chinese cities.

Chinese stone rubbings are the most appropriate souvenirs of China's former capital. Xi'an has the country's best collection of steles, or inscribed stone tablets, most of the them in the Forest of Steles (see page 89). The rubbings of memorials, calligraphy, pictures and even maps, are produced by laying paper on top of a stele, and then pounding it with a tightly-wrapped ink-filled cloth formed into a kind of mallet. It is often possible to see this being done, either at the Forest of Steles or at a handicraft factory. An expert job from a famous stone can cost hundreds, even thousands of *yuan*. On the other hand a quick rubbing from a reproduction stone could cost less than 5 *yuan*. They are on sale almost everywhere the tourist sets his foot.

The **Friendship Store,** obligatory stop on the CITS tour, is in Nanxin Jie. It boasts a total of 8000 different items on sale, everything from T-shirts to replicas of Qin soldiers. The local Chinese are forbidden to enter, and foreigners are asked to pay with foreign currency certificates instead of ordinary Chinese money. The **Arts and Crafts Store** is on the opposite side of the road, also selling to tourists.

The main shopping street is Dong Dajie (East Avenue), particularly the section between Nanxin Jie and the Bell Tower. The **Dong Dajie Department Store,** which sells a range of everyday goods including clothing, is on the corner of Nanxin Jie, right next to the Friendship Store.

Further along Dong Dajie are the **Foreign Languages Bookshop, Xinhua Bookshop** (for publications in Chinese), shops selling posters, clocks, sunglasses and an interesting one selling plants and flowers (unusual in China). Not all the shops display street numbers but the last mentioned is at number 331 Dong Dajie. There are also restaurants, snack-bars and fruit and vegetable stalls.

Just round the corner, and opposite the Bell Tower, is a **Chinese opera costume shop** supplying the municipal and county opera troupes of Shaanxi Province with embroidered silk costumes, elaborate head-dresses, hats, false beards and whiskers and odd props. Its address is 488 Dongfeng Lu. There is another opera shop in Xi Dajie (West Avenue).

Another important shopping area is around Jiefang Lu, in the northeast of the walled city. There are two department stores, the **Jiefang Lu** and the **Minsheng.** Markets selling everyday goods can be found in the area round the Bell Tower or clustered round the East, South, or North Gates.

The Xi'an branch of China International Travel Service encourages tourist groups to visit the workshops and showrooms of a number of small handicraft enterprises. Quality varies, none of the factories is particularly old, but some of the craft techniques employed are interesting.

The **Cloisonné Factory** of Xi'an which employs some 400 workers is at 21 Yanta Lu, near the Big Goose Pagoda. The **Jade Carving Factory** of Xi'an is at 173 Xiyi Lu, round the corner from the Friendship Store. Some 250 workers carve jadeite, amethyst, crystal, many other semi-precious stones, and petrified wood. Attached to the factory is a unit making rubbings from reproductions of stones in the Forest of Steles. The **Xi'an Special Arts and Crafts Factory** on Huangcheng Xi Lu, just north of the West Gate, makes sculptures and raised pictures using sea-shells, feathers, silk and other materials together with inlaid woodwork. There is another arts and crafts factory near the Big Goose Pagoda which opened in May 1981. This specializes in paintings and calligraphy, also scroll hanging, and miniature reproductions of the figures at the Qin Terracotta Army Museum.

Other interesting items worth looking for include local pottery for everyday use, basketware, embroidery, leather silhouette shadow puppets, papercuts, stuffed toys, brightly coloured pottery cows and micro-carvings on pieces of ivory no bigger than a grain of rice.

Food and Drink

In Xi'an the fare is plain and provincial, although good food is available for those who search it out. Street-stall cooking is often better than that offered by the restaurants, which is itself usually better than the routine productions of the hotels.

In country areas of Shaanxi Province (of which Xi'an is the capital) people eat noodles and steamed bread in preference to rice. Sheep are raised in the north of the province and mutton is an important source of protein. Eating habits throughout the northwest of China have been strongly influenced by the *Hui*, Chinese-speaking Muslims who of course do not eat pork. Their food can be sampled at the stalls around the Drum Tower, especially in the early evening. The best-known, best-loved dish is called *kaoyangrou*, spicy barbequed mutton. One skewer normally costs 1 *mao* (10 *fen*). Boiled mutton ravioli served in spicy sauce, *yangrou shuijiao*, costs 3 *mao* (30 *fen*) a bowl and can be found in the same area.

The most popular local dish, also *Hui* in origin, is the hearty *yangrou paomo*. Few tourists have tried it. For the standard local price of about 1 *yuan*, a large bowl and two large baked flatbreads are provided. The customer breaks the bread into very small pieces and takes the bowl back to the kitchen, where a mutton and vegetable soup, with noodles, is poured over the broken pieces of bread. It is difficult to describe the taste — perhaps something like haggis stew, noodles and digestive biscuits comes closest to it.

At a relatively more sophisticated level, Xi'an has its own special delicacies served in restaurants designated to receive foreigners. Banquets start with a cold plate of *hors d'oeuvres* arranged in the shape of a phoenix, peacock or butterfly. Other dishes include fish in milk soup, served in a copper chafing dish (*guozi yu*), coin-shaped egg and hair vegetable (*jinqian facai*), sliced pig tripe and duck gizzard (*cuan shuang cui*), whole, crispy 'calabash' chicken (*hulu ji*), and braised quail (*tiepa anchun*). Chinese

wolfberry and white fungus in soup (gouqi dun yiner) is a tonic, particularly good for the lungs.

Sweet dishes offered in ordinary eating establishments tend to be sugary, starchy and filled with red bean, peanuts or baihe, lily bulb. A number of different cakes and biscuits are on sale. There are crystal cakes (shuijing bing) and egg-thread cakes (dansi bing), amongst others.

The leading brand of liquor is called Xifeng, a colourless spirit made in Liulin Village, near Fengxiang about 90 odd miles (145 km) west of Xi'an. Another local drink is the Yellow Osmanthus Thick Wine (Huanggui choujiu). Both are said to owe their origin to alcoholic drinks of the Tang period. Xi'an has two varieties of its own beer. That with the blue label is presumably better, as it is marked 'special quality', but it is hard to tell the difference between them.

Restaurants in Xi'an are open from around 11am to 1pm for lunch, and 5 to 7pm for dinner. In the first four places listed below the standard charge for an ordinary meal for a foreigner is 10 yuan (1983). Banquets are two or three times that figure.

Restaurants

西安饭庄　东大街菊花园口
Xi'an Restaurant Intersection of Dong Dajie (East Avenue) and Juhuayuan tel. 22127
The premier restaurant of the city occupies a large modern block with six floors containing 14 dining rooms. There is little discernible ambience. Food is officially Shaanxi-style, and many of the delicacies mentioned above are available; however, the chefs are flexible and can cook other kinds of Chinese cuisine. Foreigners eat on the third floor. The calligraphy of the sign in front of the building is by Guo Moruo, a literary eminence of the People's Republic who died a few years ago.

东亚饭店　骡马市街
East Asia Restaurant Luomashi Jie tel. 28410
All the chefs in this restaurant, which is near the Bell Tower, were originally from Shanghai, and officially they prepare the cuisine of Suzhou and Wuxi, cities in southern Jiangsu Province, close to Shanghai. In practice most of the food is local in style. They serve their own 'East Asia' hotpot (Dongya huoguo), a close relative of the 'Mongolian' hotpot. Other dishes which might be tried include 'snow pagoda white fungus' (xueta yiner), 'quadruple treasures beancurd' (sibao doufu) and an almond blancmange (xingren doufu).

西安川菜馆 解放路
Xi'an Sichuan Restaurant Jiefang Lu tel. 24736
This restaurant serves authentic Sichuanese food, which is characteristically hot and spicy. Their 'Pock-marked Grandma Chen's Beancurd' (*mapo doufu*), named after the lady who invented it, eel in garlic sauce (*dasuan shanyu*) and chicken diced with chilli (*mala jiding*) are excellent. Foreigners eat on the second floor.

五一饭店 东大街
May the First Restaurant Dong Dajie (East Avenue) tel. 24410
This restaurant also caters for parties of tourists, who eat on the third floor. It specializes in the Huaiyang-style cuisine of the Anhui-Jiangsu area, although most of the food is local in flavour.

和平餐厅 大差市
Peace Restaurant Dachashi tel. 24726
This is the city's Peking-style restaurant, offering Peking duck, Mongolian hotpot, and Chinese-style hot toffee apple.

清雅饭馆 东大街
Qingya Restaurant Dong Dajie (East Avenue)
This is a Muslim restaurant which has so far had little experience of serving foreigners although there are plans eventually to open it to tourists. It is on the south side of Dong Dajie (East Avenue), a little west of the Dong Dajie Department Store going towards the Bell Tower.

新中华 东大街
New China Snacks Dong Dajie (East Avenue)
Between the Dong Dajie Department Store and the Qingya Restaurant (see above), on the south side of the road, is a small but typical sweet snack shop. Everything is very cheap and the only way to order is to point. Fried glutinous rice, covered with sugar and containing red bean, is one favourite. Another is sweet congee, rice gruel in syrup with peanuts or *baihe*, lily bulb.

白云章牛羊肉饺子馆 东大街菊花园口
Baiyunzhang Beef and Mutton Ravioli House Intersection of Dong Dajie (East Avenue) and Juhuayuan tel. 28663
Located very close to the Xi'an Restaurant, this is the place to try one of the most celebrated ordinary dishes of north China, *jiaozi*, whose nearest western equivalent is the Italian ravioli. *Jiaozi* can be prepared and cooked in a number of different ways but essentially are made of hard-wheat pasta filled with chopped meat and vegetable.

德发长饺子馆 钟楼
Defazhang Ravioli House Bell Tower tel. 26453
This also serves the mouth-watering *jiaozi*.

同德祥牛羊肉泡馍馆 社会路口
Tongdexiang Niu Yangrou Paomo House Shehui Lu entrance
tel. 22170
This is the place where the *yangrou paomo*, described in the previous
section, is served. The restaurant also serves a beef variation of the noodle
soup.

Entertainment and the Arts

The Performing Arts

Xi'an is the home of a number of professional performing arts organizations,
serving both the city and the Shaanxi countryside. The city also has its own
Conservatory of Music (at Daxingshan Temple Park), a provincial Opera
School attached to an Institute of Opera in Wenyi Road, as well as its own
film studios near the Big Goose Pagoda.

The **Shaanxi Acrobatics Troupe,** which includes conjurors, is very
popular with local people. Together with most of the various performing
arts groups, this is based near Wenyi Road, just south of the walled city.
Close by is the building of the **Shaanxi Song and Dance Troupe.** This
company is known for its vocal, orchestral and instrumental performances
of both Chinese and western music. Its stars are the singers Miss Yuan
Enming and the svelte Miss Feng Jianxue, remarkable for the élan with
which she renders western light classical, international folk and Chinese
operatic pieces, as well as her frequent changes of costume. There is a
popular flute player called Gao Ming and an *erhu* Chinese fiddle player
called Wu Tong.

The **Xi'an Song and Dance Troupe** concentrates on western ballet
and Chinese traditional dance. Like the Shaanxi troupe it has its own
orchestra. It is also located south of the walled city, although it performs in
many different places. Xi'an also has the **Shaanxi Puppet Group,** and a
troupe specializing in Chinese traditional storytelling and comic dialogues.

There are eight big theatres in the city, the most important of which is
the **People's Theatre** on Bei Dajie (North Avenue). This is mainly used
for concerts, dancing and the Peking opera (performed by the **Shaanxi
Number One** and **Shaanxi Number Two Opera Companies**).

The visitor with limited time to sample the range of entertainment in
Xi'an might just settle for a performance of the celebrated local *Qinqiang*
opera of Shaanxi Province itself.

رسول الله يا قارئ شهادة عدلين ثلاثين فان غم عليكم ثلاثين فان غم عليكم اى فان خفى عليكم هلال رمضان
وعدوا شعبان ثلاثين ثم صوموا ثم صوموا رمضان وقول عليه السلام لا تقدموا هذا الشهر بالصيام
اذا رأيتموه فافطروا فان غم عليكم فأتموا ثلاثين يوما والراوى ابو هريرة رضى وعزاه مرة رضى
لا ان يوافق ذلك صوما كان يصومه صوموا الرؤيته وافطروا للرؤيته فان غم عليكم فعدوا وذلك
وكذا وهكذا وهكذا والشهر هكذا وهكذا وهكذا وخنسرابهما مع المرة الثالثة ويفسر هذا الحديث
والقراءة من غير الكتاب منسوب الى امة العرب لا يعرفون الكتابة والقراءة يعنى نخرج جما
علم النجوم وسير القمر ولا نوءها والشهر بحساب النجوم بل نعد بعض الشهر تسعة وعشرين
عدة يوم تسعة وعشرين من السر المتقدم نحكم بدخول الشهر وان رأيناه بعد مضى ثلاثين
يكون الشهر تسعة وعشرين وشهر وعشرين على السوية والتعاقب لان قد يكون شهران ثلاثين وقد
عة وعشرين وقد يكون بعضها ثلاثين من غير تعيين فيوما ما اتفق قوله هكذا اشار تم الى الاصابع العد
ذا التفسير وبهذا التفسير تبين خطا من يعرف دخول الشهر وخروجه بآية والقمر قد رأيناه لا زال
الغرض خالفه فقد سعاه سعوا عظيما وخسر خسرانا مبينا واما الانار المجتمعة فربعد وا
عباس انه قال فرجعوت منزل الشام قال ثبت ابن عباس وهو بمكة فقال لحم متى رأيتم الهلال فقالت
الا تكتفى برؤيته معاوية واحد ... هفان هذا امر يا النبى بان نصوم اذا ايا الهلال وافط
من الغد فمام اهل العراق ثلاثين يدما وصام اهل الرجل تسعة وعشرين يوما فليس على الرجل قضاء
النبى عم قال اذا رأيتم الهلال صوموا واذا رأيتم الهلال فافطروا فان غم لصام اهل العراق بغير
انه كان دخل على عايشة يوم الشك فاتى بلبن فقلت ابى لصيام فقالت عايشة قد هو عزر

China has over 300 forms of local theatre, and *Qinqiang* is one of the oldest, most vigorous and most influential of them. It is almost certainly the original form of clapper opera, with which it is synonymous. In this style of Chinese opera, popular today throughout much of northern China, time is beaten with large wooden clap boards looking like oversized castenets. Those used in Xi'an have traditionally been made of date wood.

Xi'an city has two **Qinqiang Companies.** The drama is performed in local Xi'an dialect, with its own characteristic, rather loud, vocal style, accompanied by string instruments. It has its own conventions regarding costume and make-up. Individual operas are often three or four hours long with rapidly developed plots using all the dramatic devices found in Shakespearian comedies — abrupt changes in fortune, mistaken identities, men dressed as women, women dressed as men, both as animals (notably predatory, acrobatic tigers). Drag parts in which comedians take off vulgar, meddlesome old ladies are often star roles.

Despite its stylization, Chinese opera presents a riveting dramatic spectacle. However, foreigners and Chinese who do not understand the local dialect need to have an outline of the story in their heads before arriving at the theatre. Performances are advertized in the local newspapers, the *Xi'an Daily* and the *Shaanxi Daily.*

Peasant Painting

Hu County (Huxian), about 25 miles (40 km) southwest of the city, is the home of a celebrated school of amateur peasant painters.

The first paintings, based on the style of traditional New Year posters, were done in 1958 to record progress on the construction of a new reservoir. These were a great success, inspiring the organization of a series of art classes for the local people. During the mid-1970s there were about 2000 active painters in the county.

The Hu County paintings are bright and optimistic, many of them celebrating the fruits of labour. Their most distinctive feature is the multi-cellular design into which most of the best pictures are organized. A selection was exhibited in London and Stockholm in 1976, and many examples are on permanent display at the **Huxian Peasant Painting Exhibition Hall.**

Flora and Fauna

During the Tang Dynasty horticulture flourished in the capital Chang'an (present-day Xi'an). One of its citizens was the most celebrated gardener of Chinese history, the hunchback 'Camel' Guo. He is supposed to have grown golden peaches and propagated lotus with deep blue flowers by soaking the seeds in indigo dye.

The inhabitants of the capital were especially proud of their tree peonies, which became something of a mania, and blooms were sold for huge sums in the Chang'an Flower Market. The most popular colours were pale pink and deep purple. Tree peonies had been cultivated from about the fifth century onwards, originally in either Shaanxi or Sichuan. (The plant did not finally reach Europe until 1789 when the first one was found a home in London's Kew Gardens.) The best peony garden was at Da Cien Temple, the temple of the Big Goose Pagoda (see page 67). There is no peony garden there today, but appropriately this is the location of the **Xi'an Botanical Garden** (telephone 51720).

In the second century BC, an envoy of Emperor Han Wudi (140 – 86 BC) to central Asia brought the pomegranate tree back to China. Today the hillsides around Lintong County, including the slopes of the Mausoleum of the First Emperor of Qin, are covered in May and June with the red and white flowers of the pomegranate. The fruit grown in Xi'an and especially Lintong, 9 miles (15 km) to the east, is considered the best in the country, giving rise to the saying that 'When you think of Lintong, you think of pomegranates'.

The first attempt to catalogue the animals, birds and reptiles of Shaanxi according to western science was made in 1908 – 9. Robert Stirling Clark of New York led an expedition of 36 men, including the ornithologist Arthur de C Sowerby of the Smithsonian.

It is interesting that Sowerby records seeing pink, grey and white 'Chinese' ibises, as did a later British traveller Violet Cressy-Marcks in 1938. These wading birds, members of the stork family, are properly called Japanese ibis, though they are called *toki* in Japan. The long-beaked birds are distinguished by the bright red colouring of the side of the head and of the legs. The adult grows to a length of about 2½ feet (77 cm), head to tail.

They were formerly spread throughout east and northeast China, Korea and Japan, but apparently environmental changes in the 20th century were disastrous for the species. They declined in numbers and altogether disappeared after 1964. By 1980 there were only two known pairs left in the world. These were at the Toki Protection Centre on Japan's Sado Island. They had not reproduced for four years, and artificial incubation had failed. Then, that same year, Chinese zoologists found two nesting pairs in Shaanxi. They were discovered at Yangxian County in the Qinling Mountains. Three young were hatched that year in what is now the Qinling Number One Ibis Colony.

By comparison with the ibis, the giant panda is a relatively prolific endangered species. There are still about 1000 of these large black and white, high-altitude living, bamboo-munching 'cat-bears'. Most of them are in the neighbouring province of Sichuan; a few unlucky, if pampered, ones play star roles in world zoos. In Shaanxi Province there is one special nature reserve for them at Foping County, southwest of Xi'an and not far from the Qinling Ibis Colony.

The orange snub-nosed monkey, also known as the golden-haired monkey, is another inhabitant of the Qinling Mountains. Found in birch forests and mountain gullies, at around 8000 to 10,000 feet (2500 – 3000 m), these very agile acrobatic animals have bright yellow-orange fur, with white chests, long tails and distinctive blue circles around their eyes.

Reeves's pheasant is the original proud possessor of the long, waving tail feathers worn by generals in Chinese opera. The tail of the male reaches to 3½ to 4½ feet long (100 – 140 cm). The bird is found in mountain forests, between 2000 and 6500 feet (600 – 2000 metres) above sea level.

The **Xi'an Zoo** in Jinhua Bei Lu (tel. 31502) has examples of both giant and lesser pandas, pheasants and orange snub-nosed monkeys as well as northeast China tigers, leopards, Sichuan parrots, wild donkeys and other animals indigenous to China. There are also a number of animals presented to the Xi'an Zoo by the Japanese cities of Kyōto and Nara, with which Xi'an has a formal as well as a historical relationship. The Zoo was established in Revolution Park in 1956, but moved to a much larger site to the east in 1976. It is planned to rearrange the enclosures in the shape of the map of Shaanxi Province, with the giant pandas occupying a new, more salubrious, home.

Until surveys are published of the complete fauna of southern Shaanxi we will not have a complete inventory of species. Violet Cressy-Marcks (later to interview Mao Zedong in Yan'an, see Recommend Reading, page 91) records that in 1938 in an area 20 miles from the city she saw 'common jay, Chinese jay, blue magpie, golden eagle, pheasants, green woodpeckers, flocks of bustard, wild horned sheep and wild ducks and I was told there were leopards but I did not see any'. Near Xi'an 'there were many sulphur bellied rats, wood and field mice, also mallard, teal, wrens, redstarts, minks and goral'. At Lintong she saw 'geese, ducks, hares, snipe, bustard and mallard'. The wildlife of the Wei River plain is almost certainly much depleted now, in contrast to that of the mountains to the south.

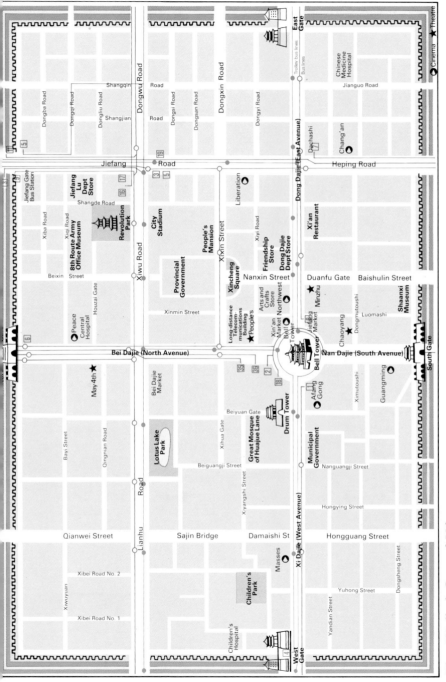

The Walled City of Xi'an

Places of Interest in the Xi'an Area
Period One: From Prehistory to 771 BC

Background

Xi'an, capital of Shaanxi Province, lies a few miles south of the Wei River, a western tributary of the Yellow River. Near the modern city is the ancient site of Chang'an (Everlasting Peace), which served as the capital of several ruling dynasties spanning a period of over 1000 years. But the Wei Valley had been settled much earlier.

Palaeolithic Before the present landscape of the Wei Valley was created from deposits of sand blown from the Mongolian Plateau, early ancestors of man lived in the area. During 1963 – 6 a skull (now in Beijing), jaw and various other bones of Lantian Man, a form of *Homo erectus* dating to around 800,000 BC, were discovered 27 miles (about 38 km) southeast of Xi'an.

In the spring of 1978 an almost complete skull was found of what is now known as Dali Man in Dali County, near the provincial border with Shanxi. He is thought to belong to an early subspecies of *Homo sapiens*, living in perhaps 300,000 or 200,000 BC.

Neolithic The development of agriculture found an ideal setting in the Wei and Middle Yellow River Valleys, with their deep loess deposit containing all the necessary minerals for successful cultivation. From approximately 5000 BC onwards settlements were formed, larger and more permanent than similar ones elsewhere in the world. The early Neolithic stage in China is called the Yangshao Culture. The name Painted Pottery Culture is sometimes preferred, which contrasts with the Black Pottery, or Longshan Culture which followed it. Yangshao Culture lasted until around 3000 BC. A typical Yangshao or Painted Pottery Culture settlement has been excavated at Banpo, within a few miles of Xi'an.

Sights

Banpo Museum

The 1953 discovery of a New Stone Age village, at Banpo, less than five miles (about 7 km) east of Xi'an, has been described as the 'greatest single contribution to prehistoric archaeology in east Asia' (John Hay, *Ancient China*). Dating from approximately 5000 to 4000 BC, it is the most complete example of an agricultural neolithic settlement anywhere in the world. Its remarkably well-preserved condition makes it a major attraction for visitors to Xi'an.

The site can be reached by bus 8 from the Bell Tower or trolleybus 5 from Dongwu Road.

An area of one acre (4000 sq m) has been fully excavated, enclosed and put on view to the public. Foundations of 45 houses have been uncovered. Some have floors at ground level, some above; some are round, some square. The largest dwelling may have been a communal meeting place, or alternatively the house of the chief. There are also two exhibition halls with notes in impeccable English accompanying the excavated articles displayed.

From the implements and utensils unearthed, archaeologists have learned a great deal about the daily life of Banpo. It was a typical Yangshao Culture community. Between two and three hundred people lived there, practising slash-and-burn agriculture. They depended on millet and pork for their existence. In addition to millet, they planted vegetables such as cabbage and mustard, and hemp which was used to make clothing. Besides pigs, they kept dogs and perhaps chickens and other animals. They also hunted and fished. They fired and painted extraordinarily beautiful red clay pots with both abstract and non-abstract designs.

Chinese archaeologists believe that a primitive communist matriarchal clan lived at Banpo. In the communal burial ground found to the north of the site, men and women were buried seperately, usually by themselves, sometimes in multiple single-sex graves. Women were generally interred with a greater number of funeral objects than men. However, it has been pointed out by foreign archaeologists that in most early matriarchal settlements, excavated elsewhere, whole families related through the female line have been found buried together.

Remains of the Capitals of the Western Zhou

Bronze metallurgy was practised from about the middle of the millenium, contemporary with the emergence of the Shang. (This dynasty had the first historically authentic line of kings). During the Shang period (c.1600 — 1027 BC) the Wei and Jing Valleys were dominated by a relatively backward people called the Zhou. Under their leader, King Wu, they attacked and captured Anyang, the capital of the Shang, in 1027 BC. The Zhou Dynasty lasted formally until 249 BC, but the kings only enjoyed real power until 771 BC. This period is called the Western Zhou. Archaeologists have discovered the remains of two Zhou palaces west of Xi'an, at Fengchu Village, Qishan County, and at Zhaochen Village, Fufeng County.

A **Western Zhou chariot burial pit** was unearthed at **Zhangjiapo,** Chang'an County in 1955. The war chariot was the pre-eminent symbol of power in the Bronze Age. One of the pits excavated at Zhangjiapo contained two chariots and the remains of six horses and one slave, interred as part of the funeral of a lord. These are on display in a small museum.

It is recorded that the Zhou established five different capitals in the Wei and Jing Valleys at different times. Two of these have been identified.

Fengjing on the western bank of the Feng River was an early capital. **Haojing** on the opposite bank was the capital from 1027 to 771 BC. The sites have been excavated and the remains of houses, workshops, burials and some hoards of bronze articles have been found.

Xi'an in relation to Former Cities

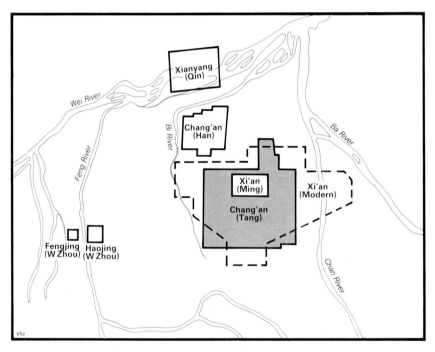

Period Two: Feudal China 770 to 207 BC

Background

The Rise of Qin The Eastern Zhou began with the re-establishment of the capital near Luoyang, Henan Province in 770 BC. The dynasty is divided into two periods, the Spring and Autumn Annals and the Warring States, both taken from the names of books. During the former the Zhou kings were only nominal leaders and the Chinese world was divided into more than 100 petty principalities; by the beginning of the latter, these had been absorbed into seven much larger states.

The Warring States period saw the beginning of the Iron Age in China, a time of tremendous technological progress in the arts of both war and peace. In due course Qin (Ch'in) became the most powerful of the contending states, and flourished as the result of a single-minded emphasis on military prowess, public works and food production.

The First Emperor In 246 BC King Zheng came to the Qin throne, a boy of 13. During his reign Qin superiority was finally established when the six other states were annexed between 230 and 221 BC, creating the first Chinese empire.

King Zheng took the title of Qin Shihuàngdi, First Emperor of Qin. (The term *huangdi* had previously only been used for deities and mythological hero-rulers such as the Yellow Emperor. Qin itself is the origin of our word China.) His capital was at Xianyang (see page 43), northeast of the present-day town, on the north bank of the Wei River. On his accession in 246 BC he began supervising the construction of his mausoleum (see below).

Sights

Qin Ling, the Mausoleum of the First Emperor

The Qin Ling and the Terracotta Army Museum lie some 18 miles (30 km) east of Xian and are quite easily reached by public transport. Every hour until noon buses leave from a side street near the railway station, stopping to pick up passengers at Banpo. (See page 22 for details on tour buses.)

The construction of the First Emperor's palace of death began on his accession as king in 246 BC. Work intensified after the conquest of the rival states with 700,000 labourers conscripted to work on it. The site chosen was south of the Wei River beside the slopes of Black Horse Mountain in what is now Lintong County, 18 miles (30 km) from Xi'an. The outside of the mausoleum is in the form of a low earth pyramid with a wide base. Preliminary investigation by the Chinese has confirmed that there were an inner and an outer enclosure. The mausoleum has not been excavated.

Ancillary tombs of five men and two women have recently been discovered near the mausoleum. The occupants were probably victims of the Second Emperor in the power struggle following the death of Qin Shihuangdi. In addition, the graves of a general and of some 70 Qin labourers have been found together with large numbers of horse skeletons. None of the sites of these finds has so far (1983) been put on view to the public.

The body of the First Emperor, Qin Shihuangdi, was interred in 209 BC, a year after his death. His childless wives were also buried alive in the tomb, together with artisans who had knowledge of the inner structure of the mausoleum. It was plundered — to what extent we still do not know — by a rebel general called Xiang Yu (Hsiang Yü) in 206 BC.

Information about the construction of the mausoleum comes almost entirely from the brush of Sima Qian (Ssu-ma Ch'ien), the author of *The Historical Records*, China's first large-scale work of history which was written about a century after the fall of Qin.

According to Sima, heaven and earth were represented in the central chamber of the tomb. The ceiling formed the sky with pearls for stars. The floor was a physical map of the world in stone; the 100 rivers of the empire flowed mechanically with mercury. All manner of treasures were piled inside for the emperor's opulent afterlife. Crossbows were set up and positioned to shoot automatically if the interior was disturbed. After it was sealed the tomb was grassed over to appear as a natural hill.

The discovery of the terracotta army (see below) has since contributed further to this picture of the emperor's magnificent burial arrangements. Their colossal scale seems a fitting memorial to the man who first unified China. Qin Shihuangdi, who has been called both tyrant and reformer, ruled over a vast territory. Having abolished the feudal system completely, he was the sole source of power and final authority for a centralised government in Xianyang. The government administered a severe legal code, taxed the people, and conscripted labour for both military and civil projects. To safeguard the northern frontier, the existing defensive lines along the border were rebuilt and extended to become China's Great Wall. An army was sent to the extreme south, the northern part of today's Vietnam. Roads, irrigation schemes, palaces and above all the First Emperor's mausoleum all required hordes of reluctant labourers. Out of a total population of 20 million, 1½ million are thought to have been called to some form of service to the State. At the same time, independent thought was suppressed: books whose contents were considered subversive were burned, and hundreds of scholars were buried alive. These oppressive policies caused suffering on a huge scale, and on Qin Shihuangdi's death 11 years after taking the imperial title, revolts swiftly followed.

Qin Terracotta Army Museum

During a drought in the spring of 1974 the Xiyang Production Brigade of Yanzhai Commune decided to sink a well at a spot less than a mile (1.5 km) east of the First Emperor's mausoleum, which happened to be exactly at right angles to the centre of the original outer enclosure. They came upon, in the words of *Newsweek*, 'the clay clones of an 8000-man army'. When the first figures were unearthed it was not appreciated how many there were, but gradually the significance of the discovery was realized: the emperor had decided to take an army with him to the afterworld.

The Qin Terracotta Army Museum, which opened in 1979, is a large hangar-like building constructed over Pit Number One, the place of the original discovery in 1974. There are two exhibition halls outside the main building. The terracotta figures were found 16 feet (5 m) below the surface in a vault. The vault was originally built with walls of pounded earth, and a wooden roof was added before the enclosure was sealed. It appears that the troops of General Xiang Yu, who had plundered the Qin Ling, opened the vault in 206 BC and set fire to the roof, which collapsed, smashing the terracottas in situ.

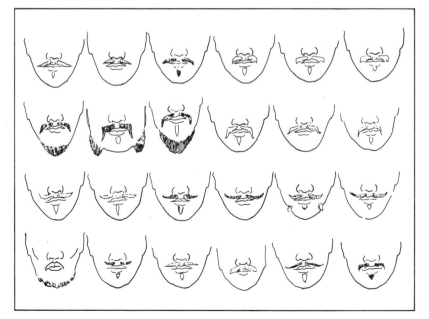

The mustachios of Qin — the varied faces of the soldiers of the Qin terracotta army. (from Kaogu yu wenwu, No 3 1980, Xi'an)

Terracotta Troops The terracotta soldiers are realistic and vigorous pieces of sculpture. Each soldier's face has individual features, prompting speculation that they were modelled from life. They have squarish faces with broad foreheads and large, thick-lipped mouths, and they wear neat moustaches, sometimes beards. Expressions are generally austere, eyes focussed far ahead. The figures are mostly 5 feet 11 inches (1.8 m) in height. The lower part of the body is solid, the upper hollow. They were originally painted, but the colour has now been almost entirely lost.

The soliders are divided into infantry armed with swords and spears, archers, crossbow archers, cavalry, chariot drivers and officers. The chariots no longer exist except for their metal fittings. They were almost certainly real ones, made of wood. Each is drawn by four pottery horses, on average 4 feet 11 inches tall (1.5 m) by 6 feet 7 inches (2 m) long.

The terracotta troops bear real arms, made of bronze. A huge number has been unearthed: swords, daggers, billhooks, spears, halberds, axes, crossbow triggers and arrowheads. The copper-tin alloy used was combined with 11 other elements such as nickel, magnesium, cobalt and chrome, and many weapons have emerged sharp, shiny and untarnished. The arrowheads contain a poisonous percentage of lead.

The Excavations Pit Number One has 11 parrallel corridors running from east to west, between larger open spaces at either end. The soldiers face east in battle formation. Three rows, each of 70 lightly-armed archers, form the vanguard. They are followed by 38 columns of more heavily-armed infantry interspersed with war chariots. A single column of spearmen face north, south and west respectively. From the evidence of test excavations it is thought that there may be more than 6000 pieces of pottery in total.

An L-shaped vault, now called Pit Number Two, was found northeast of Number One in May 1976. It contained nearly 1000 terracottas, including four chariots, cavalrymen leading their mounts, crossbow archers and foot soldiers. One figure 6 feet 5 inches (1.95 m) in height is considered to be a general. A number of figures were removed before the vault was refilled with earth.

Another small vault, Pit Number Three, was unearthed beside Number two in June 1976. Only containing one chariot and 68 guards, this is thought to represent the army headquarters. The vault has also been filled in again.

Bronze Chariots In 1981 it was revealed that two, then three more, half life-sized bronze chariots had been found, the earliest ever discovered in China. They were unearthed 56 feet (17 m) west of the mausoleum. They were discovered in good condition and are of the highest artistic standards of the Qin period. Each chariot is drawn by four horses, 2 feet 4 inches (72 cm) high by 3 feet 3 inches (1 m) in length. Originally painted white, cm) high by 3 feet 3 inches (1 m) in length. Originally painted white, now turned to grey, they bear harnesses inlaid with gold and silver. Each quadriga has a bronze carriage with an awning of thin sheet bronze, painted with cloud and geometric patterns. The drivers of the original pair are dressed as ninth grade officials. One stands 3 feet (91 cm) high, while the other is sitting. It is believed that the figures were first modelled in clay and then cast in bronze. They may be part of a procession.

Equally astounding treasures probably lie north, south and west of the mausoleum; but Chinese archaeologists have remained tight-lipped in the face of such speculations, and it is not likely that any further discoveries will be published until thorough examinations have taken place.

Remains of Xianyang

The Qin capital Xianyang was built in 350 BC on the north bank of the Wei River. It is said to have developed into a metropolis with 800,000 inhabitants before rebel general Xiang Yu set fire to it in 206 BC.

In 1961 the exact location of the city was re-discovered in the Yaodian People's Commune about 10 miles (15 km) northwest of Xi'an.

Excavations in the 1960s and 1970s revealed the foundations of the Xianyang Palace, the First Emperor's principal domicile, partly built on a terrace of pounded earth. The structure and the function of different parts of the palace are now known. Important discoveries were made including the remains of some murals. Building materials, decorated bricks and tiles were found in large quantities.

Remains of Afang Palace

In 212 BC the First Emperor decided to build a new and larger principal palace on the other side of the Wei River, some six miles (10 km) west of Xi'an. Afang Palace was never finished, but the raised platform of pounded earth has remained to this day.

(preceding page) Stone animal sculptures at the tomb of Huo Qubing, Western Han Dynasty general

Period Three: The Han Dynasty 206 BC to AD 220

Background

The Qin Dynasty maintained its authority only until 209 BC. The First Emperor's death was followed by outbreaks of rebellion and civil war, which led to the empire's dissolution. The Qin forces were defeated by General Xiang Yu in 207 BC. The general himself was overthrown four years later by the founder of the Han Dynasty.

The first Han emperor was a general of plebeian background called Liu Bang (Liu Pang), known posthumously by his dynastic title of Han Gaozu (Han Kao-tsu), which literally means Great-great-grandfather of Han. His capital, called Chang'an, was built in the strategic Wei Valley. Accordingly the first half of Han rule, lasting until AD 8, is called the Western Han to distinguish it from the Eastern Han period, 25 – 220, when the captial was at Luoyang.

The Capital City of Chang'an

In 202 BC Liu Bang moved into a minor Qin palace on the southern side of the Wei. Later the architect Xiao He added a large new complex of some 40 buildings to the west of it. This was the Weiyang Palace (see page 50) which was to remain the principal seat of the Western Han emperors. Together these two palaces formed the nucleus of Han Dynasty Chang'an.

The imperial establishment soon outgrew the two original palaces and more buildings were added during the time of the Emperor Han Huidi (reigned 194 – 187 BC). An irregular-shaped wall was built around the palaces, eventually forming a circumference of about 14 miles (22 km). Within the wall there were eight main streets and 160 alleys, and a central drainage system served the city. Outside the wall another city was growing too, that of the artisans with markets, workshops and houses.

The Silk Road It was during the Han that central and western Asia was opened up to the Chinese. This was to have a profound impact on Chang'an.

From the capital Han Wudi, the Martial Emperor) (reigned 140 – 86 BC), launched a series of campaigns against the Xiongnu, the warlike Turkish people of the steppes, who were a constant threat to the northern frontier of China. In 139 BC Zhang Qian (Chang Ch'ien) was sent officially to central Asia to find allies against the Xiongnu. On his second journey in 119 BC he went as far as the Ili Valley, on the present-day border with the Soviet Union, and from there despatched envoys to India and the Iranian Empire as well as kingdoms east of the Caspian Sea. One of the sights Zhang Qian reported were the fine horses in what is now Soviet Uzbekistan. A stock of the horses was brought to China, and these were later the inspiration of Chinese sculptors, painters and writers to an extent that was almost obsessional, especially during the Tang Dynasty.

Merchant caravans followed the armies and established the routes of what Europeans later called the Silk Road. The eastern section opened by the Chinese linked up with trade routes in western Asia to form lines of trade and cultural exchange stretching from Chang'an to the Mediterranean. Official contact with the Roman Empire was attempted in AD 97, but the envoy never got through. Unofficial representatives of Rome, including a party of jugglers in 120, did however arrive in Chang'an. There was a special street where foreigners were accommodated, and even a protocol department to arrange the formal side of their reception.

Paper was one of many Chinese inventions that eventually reached Europe via the Silk Road. The world's earliest pieces of paper were discovered at Ba Bridge, east of Xi'an, in 1957. It was originally thought that paper was invented during the Eastern Han, but these pieces of hemp paper were made during the reign of Han Wudi (140 – 86 BC).

The Imperial Tombs of the Western Han Dynasty

There are nine tombs of the Western Han emperors on the north bank of the Wei and two south of the present city of Xi'an. The construction of each one was started soon after the accession of the sovereign and, according to regulations, one third of all State revenues was devoted to the project. On the death of the emperor valuable objects were placed in the tomb and the body was interred in a suit of jade plates, sewn together with gold wire. A piece of jade was placed in the mouth of the emperor. Prominent members of the imperial family and important officials were buried in smaller ancillary or satellite tombs nearby. None of the imperial mausoleums has been excavated, and they remain irregular flat-topped grassy pyramids, 110 to 150 feet (33 – 46 m) above the plain.

Sights

Mao Ling, the Mausoleum of Emperor Han Wudi

In 140 BC Han Wudi (Han Wu-ti), the Martial Emperor, came to the throne he was to occupy for 54 years. Cast very much in the mould of the First Emperor of Qin, he initiated a new period of dynamic expansion. Imperial rule was extended to the southeastern coastal region of China, northern Vietnam and northern Korea. His tomb, the Mao Ling, is 25 miles (40 km) west of Xi'an. It has not been excavated.

The Martial Emperor had tried to make himself immortal. He put a bronze statue (the Brazen Immortal) in a high tower to catch the pure dew in a bowl, which he drank with powdered jade. The potion proved ineffective, and he died in his 70th year. Apparently the accumulation of treasures intended for his tomb was so great that they could not all be fitted in. It is said that live animals accompanied the burial, also many of the emperor's books.

The mausoleum was desecrated, rather than robbed, by peasant rebels called the Red Eyebrows just before the establishment of the Eastern Han. They removed articles from the tomb and threw them on a bonfire. Archaeologists believe that they have found the patch of burnt earth where this happened.

From the top of the tomb mound it is possible to scan the smaller satellite tombs, some round, some square. Some of the smaller tombs have been excavated, but none of the major ones.

The Tomb of Huo Qubing

The 'Swift Cavalry General', later Grand Marshal, Huo Qubing was born in 140 BC. His uncle took him to fight the fierce northern nomads, the Xiongnu, when he was 18. He died at the age of only 24. According to Sima Qian, who was a contemporary, the Martial Emperor built a special tomb for him in the shape of the Qilian Mountain (which marks the present-day border of Gansu and Qinghai Provinces), where Huo had won a great victory.

The tomb, less than a mile (1 km) from the emperor's, has been identified with something approaching certainty by the discovery of 16 remarkable stone sculptures. All are at the site. They are of horses (one of them apparently trampling a Xiongnu), animals including a tiger, boar, elephant and ox, and two strange human figures, perhaps demons or gods, one of which is wrestling with a bear. This last stone, about 9 feet (2.77 m) high, may represent a Xiongnu idol. Huo Qubing brought back at least one of these, known as the 'Golden Man'.

On top of the steep-sided tomb mound is a derelict little temple. This dates to the last dynasty and has no real connection with the tomb.

Museum Beside the two galleries where the stone sculptures are displayed there is a museum. The exhibits are almost all of the Western Han period and were discovered in the area of the Mao Ling.

There are a number of bronze articles, including money, agricultural implements and a magnificent rhinoceros, though the latter is now in the Shaanxi Museum and only a reproduction is on display. There are also examples of the decorated building materials for which both the Qin and Han were famous.

Remains of the Han City of Chang'an

Han City Walls The site of the Han capital is on the northwestern edge of the present-day city of Xi'an. Today, the walls are still there but within are fields of wheat and rape seed, not palaces.

Remains of Weiyang Palace The southern part of the city was excavated in 1957-9 and the layout of the palaces is known. The raised area of the audience hall of Weiyang Palace, the principal seat of the Western Han emperors, can be reached by road. The platform is 330 feet (101 m) long, much smaller than claimed for the original hall, but we know that the Weiyang was rebuilt several times during the Tang period, and it is more than possible that the foundations have been altered.

Han City Armoury Built in 200 BC, the armoury occupied 57 acres (23 hectares) near the present-day village of Daliuzhai, next to the site of Weiyang Palace. Recent excavations have revealed a large number of iron weapons, and some made of bronze. At the end of 1981 it was announced that a number of suits of armour had been found weighing 77 to 88 pounds (35 to 40 kilograms).

Period Four: The Golden Age 581 to 907
Background

The collapse of the Han Dynasty in 220 after years of insoluble economic and political problems was followed by centuries of power struggles, barbarian invasions and political fragmentation, with interludes of unity and order. In 581 a high-ranking official Yang Jian seized the throne and founded the Sui Dynasty.

The Sui and the Capital City of Daxingcheng

The old Han city of Chang'an was by then too derelict to serve as the symbol of power of the first Sui emperor, reigning with the title of Wendi (Wen-ti). He commissioned a brilliant engineer Yuwen Kai to build a new city — Daxingcheng, or the City of the Great Revival — southeast of the old one.

Yang Jian and Yuwen Kai created one of the greatest, perhaps *the* greatest of all planned cities. The huge rectangular area designated for the metropolis faced the four cardinal points and had an outer wall with a circumference of over 22 miles (36 km).

The Sui Dynasty was, however, short-lived. Wendi was succeeded by his even more ambitious son, the Emperor Sui Yangdi (Sui Yang-ti). He ordered the construction of a new capital at Luoyang, a huge programme of canal building, and a disastrous attempted invasion of Korea. Rebellions followed and the emperor was assassinated in Yangzhou in 618.

The Establishment of the Tang Dynasty

Power was seized by the Li family. Li Yuan, hereditary Duke of Tang, marched on Daxingcheng in 617 and the following year made himself emperor with the title of Tang Gaozu (T'ang Kao-tzu). The capital was renamed Chang'an, a deliberate move to assume by implication the mantle of the Han. In turn, Tang Gaozu was ousted by his second son Li Shimin, who took the throne himself with the title of Tang Taizong (T'ang T'ai-tsung), and effectively consolidated the Tang.

Empress Wu

Taizong died in 649 and was succeeded by his ninth son, who reigned with the title of Gaozong until 683. However, the next effective ruler was a woman, not a man. Wu Zetian was born in 624 and became a concubine of Taizong. On his death she withdrew from court and became a Buddhist nun, only to be recalled by Gaozong and eventually become his empress in 655.

After Gaozong's death Wu Zetian dethroned two of her sons and her official reign began in 690. Although Empress Wu's rule was characterized by recurrent palace intrigues and ruthless political murders, China prospered greatly during her reign.

For economic as well as political reasons she preferred Luoyang to Chang'an and the capital was in the former city from 683 to 701. She was finally removed from power, and the Tang re-established, when she was in her 80s just before her death in 705.

The Reign of Emperor Tang Xuanzong

The period of struggle over the Tang succession was ended through the emergence of the third great ruler of the dynasty, Emperor Xuanzong, Empress Wu's grandson. Popularly known as Ming Huang, the Enlightened Emperor, his reign corresponds with what is called the High Tang, the apogee of the most confident and cosmopolitan of all phases of Chinese civilization. The Tang empire was the largest, richest, most advanced state in the world and the centre and symbol of its glory was Chang'an, the greatest city in the world. Only the Baghdad of Hārūn al Rashīd offered any comparison. By the middle of the eighth century China had a population estimated at 53 million of which nearly 2 million lived in the capital.

The emperor presided over a brilliant, extravagant court, patronizing the greatest concentration of literary and artistic genius in Chinese history. Xuanzong's contemporaries included the paramount poets of China, Du Fu (Tu Fu, 712 – 770) and Li Bai (Li Po, 699 – 762) and the greatest of painters, Wu Daozi (Wu Tao-tzu, 700 – 760).

The High Tang ended with a tragic love affair. Yang Yuhuan, the most celebrated *femme fatale* in Chinese history, was a concubine of one of the emperor's 30 sons. The aging Emperor Xuanzong became infatuated with her; she entered the palace in 736 at the age of 18, and was given the title of Yang Guifei or Imperial Concubine Yang. While the emperor neglected state affairs for her sake, she promoted the interests of her own family and favourites.

In 755 her adopted son An Lushan, the Turkish commander of the northeast frontier, made a bid for power. The emperor and his concubine were forced to flee the capital. Some 30 miles west of the city, their imperial guard mutinied and demanded the death of the Imperial Concubine. Under duress the emperor agreed. Yang Guifei was strangled in front of Xuanzong's horse in the courtyard of a small Buddhist temple. Her tomb is still there today.

Xuanzong died a broken man in 762, having earlier abdicated in favour of his third son.

Chang'an in the Eighth Century

Chang'an in the eighth century was a lively, crowded, beautiful city. It was also a well-organized city, appropriate to its planned nature and to its role as the capital of a well-ordered society.

In the centre was the Imperial City with the Imperial Secretariat, the Imperial Chancellery, the Censorate and the Department of State Affairs under which came the Six Boards of Personnel, Revenue, Rites, War, Justice and Public Works, an organization of government which lasted, in form at least, for the next thousand years.

The Street of the Vermilion Bird, the central north–south avenue, divided the Outer City into two districts: the area of the aristocrats to the east, and the rather more populated section of the merchants and lower classes to the west. The two markets which served them were very large and highly organized. We know that the shops and workshops of the East Market were divided into 220 trades, each one with its own exclusive area, its own bazaar.

Much of the colour in Chang'an was provided by the 'westerners' — the streets thronged with merchants from central Asia and Arabia, and particularly travellers from Persia.

Central Asian fashions dominated the capital. Women dressed in the Persian style and wore exotic western jewellery. Men played polo. The various Buddhist temples and monasteries of the capital vied with each other in offering unusual and foreign, if devotional, entertainments.

Foreigners congregated in the West Market. This was a more exciting, more vulgar place than the East Market, and also the place where criminals were punished. It consisted of bazaars, workshops, merchants' houses, hostelries, taverns and places of entertainment. There was a Persian bazaar and markets selling precious jewels and pearls, spices, medicinal herbs, silk, and a whole range of everyday items, including the newly-fashionable beverage, tea. There were the shops of the unpopular Uygur (Uighur) Turkish moneylenders, and wineshops where the songs and dances of central Asia were performed. Other entertainment was provided by courtesans from the lands bordering Persia, some reputedly blond and blue-eyed.

Foreign Religions in Chang'an For much of the Tang the authorities allowed the foreign communities freedom of religion. Zoroastrianism, Manichaeism, Nestorianism and finally Islam followed Buddhism to Chang'an (see section on Buddhism pages 65 – 66).

In the Shaanxi Museum there is a tombstone, dated 874, inscribed in Chinese and Persian Pahlavi script, originally marking the grave of Ma, wife of Suren, a Zoroastrian.

In the eighth century there was one Nestorian Christian chapel in Chang'an. Another church was founded in 781; the celebrated Nestorian Stele, which records this event in Chinese and Syriac, is in the Forest of Steles attached to the Shaanxi Museum (see page 88).

The Manichees, who believed in a combination of Gnostic Christianity and Zoroastrianism, also had a place of worship in Chang'an in the eighth century.

The Influence of Chang'an If Chang'an itself was cosmopolitan, it also had unparalleled influence throughout central and eastern Asia. The royal progeny of several Korean and central Asian states, as well as Tibet, were educated in the schools and monasteries of the Tang capital. But by far the greatest transfer of Tang culture was to Japan. From the mid seventh century to the end of the ninth a whole series of official missions were sent by sea to China. The Japanese cities of Nara and Kyōto were built on the same plan as Chang'an, though naturally smaller. The regular layout of Kyōto still remains today, and the best examples of Tang wooden architecture also survive in Japan rather than China.

The Destruction of Chang'an In the ninth century Chang'an's importance waned with the Tang Dynasty itself coming under pressure as factions jostled for power. Twice Chang'an was sacked by peasant rebels and troops of the imperial forces. In 904 the Tang court was moved to Luoyang. The main surviving buildings were dismantled and the beams were taken to the Wei River where they were lashed together to form rafts which were floated down to the new capital. Between 904 and 906 the city walls were demolished and a new more modest wall was put up around the old Imperial City. In 907 the last Tang emperor was finally deposed and Chang'an was renamed Daanfu.

The Imperial Tombs of the Tang Dynasty
From the tomb of the Emperor Xuanzong in the east to the tomb of Gaozong and the Empress Wu in the west, the 18 Tang tombs are spread out in a line 75 miles (120 km) long. Most of them are set into natural hills and mountains, rather than underneath artificial mounds.

Each tomb was originally surrounded by a square wall and had a series of buildings for ceremonial purposes and for the use of the guards. Each had its own 'Imperial Way', an avenue lined with stone sculptures. The Tang conception was much grander than that of the well-known Ming Tombs in Beijing (Peking), where all 13 tombs share a common approach.

None of the underground palaces of the emperors has been excavated, but important subsidiary tombs of the Zhao Ling and the Qian Ling have been.

Sights

Zhao Ling, the Mausoleum of Emperor Tang Taizong

Zhao Ling is located in the main peak of Mount Jiuzong, approximately 40 miles (60 km) northwest of Xi'an. Although 14 of the satellite tombs have been excavated, the emperor's mausoleum is still intact. The whole necropolis covers an area of some 78 square miles (20,000 hectares). Visitors are normally taken to see the Zhao Ling Museum, but not the site on Mount Jiuzong itself.

Taizong was a great military commander, with a love of horses. Six bas-reliefs of his favourite mounts including that of his most famous horse Quanmo were originally placed at the northern entrance to the tomb. Sadly Quanmao cannot be seen in Xi'an. The stone, together with one other, is in the University Museum of Philadelphia. It was taken there in 1914. The other four stones are in the Stone Sculpture Gallery of the Shaanxi

Museum, with plaster reproductions of the two in America. The originals were broken in several places in 1918, apparently in an attempt to facilitate their transport abroad.

Museum Visitors to the Zhao Ling complex are usually taken to the museum. In the museum there is a Forest of Steles (not to be confused with the famous one at the Shaanxi Museum). This is a collection of 42 vertical memorial tablets which originally stood outside the tomb mounds, and 10 flat tablets from the interiors.

In the exhibition room, next door, are displayed all the artifacts removed from the excavated satellite tombs. There is a splendid selection of Tang funerary pottery, both glazed and unglazed, including figurines of Chinese and central Asians, horses and camels. There are some fragments of wall paintings, a ceremonial crown from a satellite tomb and a massive pottery roof finial from the Hall of Offerings, the main building of the original enclosure in front of the emperor's mausoleum.

Qian Ling, the Mausoleum of Emperor Tang Gaozong and Empress Wu Zetian

Of all the imperial tomb complexes near Xi'an the Qian Ling is probably the best preserved and the most complete. It is 53 miles (85 km) west of Xi'an. Standing at the southern approach to the mausoleum it is possible to appreciate the original Tang layout and design. It has never been robbed, or excavated, but there are interesting relics in its vicinity.

The main southern approach is between two prominent small hills, surmounted with towers built in the eighth century. Beneath them are two obelisk-like Cloud Pillars and then a series of pairs of stone statues lining the route to the mausoleum. First there are two winged horses, then two vermilion birds, appearing much like ostriches. Then five pairs of saddled horses, originally each with a groom. These are followed by ten pairs of tall, almost hieratic figures of guardians. They have very large heads, wear long-sleeved robes, and hold the hilts of long swords that rest on the ground in front of them.

Beyond the guardians are two stone memorials: the one on the left (west) commemorates the reign of Tang Gaozong and is balanced on the east side by the so-called Blank Tablet in honour of Empress Wu. The original implication was apparently that the old Empress was beyond praise, but memorials were in fact inscribed on it during the Song and Jin Dynasties (960 – 1234).

The other side (north) of the two ruined towers are 61 now headless stone figures. From inscriptions on the backs of these figures we know that they represent actual foreigners who came to the Chinese court in the seventh century. Some are envoys of central Asian countries, some are barbarian chiefs. Behind them are two powerful sculptures of stone lions, guarding the southern entrance to the original inner enclosure, now no longer extant. There are similar pairs of animals at the north, east and west entrances. Just inside the old southern entrance is an 18th-century stele.

The Qian Ling Satellite Tombs

There are 17 satellite tombs, all beneath man-made mounds, to the southeast of the principal mausoleum. The names of the 17 occupants are all known. Five of the tombs were excavated between 1960 and 1972. They had previously been robbed, but evidently only of gold, silver and precious gems. Archaeologists found a large number of pieces of pottery. However, the mural paintings in the interiors are by far the most exciting discoveries at the sites, providing information about Tang court life, and serving as examples of the quality of painting of the period.

Unfortunately although the paintings survived well enough when the tombs were sealed they started to deteriorate after the tombs had been opened. All the principal paintings have now been taken to the Shaanxi Museum, and replaced with reproductions, vigorous and fairly accurate to the originals.

The Tomb of Princess Yongtai (Yung-t'ai) This was the first tomb to be excavated. Princess Yongtai was a granddaughter of Emperor Gaozong and Empress Wu. She died in 701 at the age of 17.

According to the records she was executed by her grandmother on suspicion of having criticized some court favourites. Five years after her death her remains were exhumed and her tomb built at the Qian Ling complex. The memorial tablet inside the tomb states that she died in childbirth, perhaps because the manner of her death was considered shameful.

On excavation the skeleton of a tomb robber was discovered inside, evidently murdered by his accomplices. The modern Japanese writer Yasushi Inoue has written a short story, *Princess Yung-tai's Necklace*, based on this incident — see page 91.) The murals in the Princess's tomb represent court attendants, almost all of them women, wearing the elegant central Asian fashions of the day. The stone sarcophagus is engraved with figures, birds and flowers.

The Tomb of Prince Yide (I-te) The tomb of Princess Yongtai's half-brother, who died at the age of 19, apparently for the same reason and at the same time as his half-sister, is also dated to the same year as hers, 706.

The ceiling of Prince Yide's tomb is decorated with stars, the walls with court ladies and eunuchs, palace guards, hunting attendants and a long mural at the entrance with a 196-man procession of guards massed below the high watchtowers of a palace.

The Tomb of the Heir-Apparent Prince Zhanghuai Prince Zhanghuai was one of Empress Wu's sons. He was heir-apparent from 675

to 680, but was then disgraced by his mother and forced to commit suicide in 684, at the age of 31. His tomb was built in around 706. The two main paintings in the tomb are of a polo match on one side, and a hunting cavalcade opposite. There are also representations of foreign emissaries with court officials.

The two other tombs that have been opened are of the Prime Minister Xue Yuanzhao and General Li Jinxing. These have received little publicity and evidently do not have any murals.

Remains of Daming Palace

Daming Palace, or the Palace of Great Luminosity, was begun by Taizong in 634 for the use of his father, although Gaozu died before it was completed. In 663 it was much enlarged for Emperor Gaozong and from then on became the principal palace of the Tang emperors.

The site of Daming Palace is to the northeast of the walled city, on the fringe of the modern urban area. It is now largely fields. The terraces on which once stood Hanyuan Hall (where important ceremonies were held) and Linde Hall (another large, but informal complex) may still be seen, together with a depression which was the ornamental Penglai Pool in Tang times. The whole area was excavated between 1957 and 1959, and the foundations of some 20 buildings were discovered. The Linde Hall in particular was completely excavated, although the earth has now been filled in again.

Xingqing Park

In the beginning of the eighth century, the sons of Emperor Tang Ruizong (reigned 684 − 690, 710 − 712) lived in a ward on the eastern edge of the city. It became known as the Xingqing Palace in 714 after Emperor Xuanzong succeeded his father. Famous for its peonies, Xingqing was a favorite palace of the emperor and Imperial Concubine Yang. After the Tang, the land on which the palace had been built eventually reverted to agricultural use.

In 1958, during the Great Leap Forward, Xingqing Park covering 122 acres (50 hectares) was laid out on the site of the Tang palace. Thousands of citizens were involved in the work which took only 120 days to complete. Today it is much the most pleasant park in Xi'an, with a large ornamental lake and a number of Tang-style buildings bearing the names of famous halls and pavilions in the palace of Xuanzong. There is a white marble memorial, erected in 1979, to Abe no Nakamaro (701 − 770), a famous secular Japanese visitor to Chang'an during the Tang, who rose to become a Collator of Texts in the Imperial Library.

Huaqing Hotsprings

From the Western Zhou onwards, a series of pleasure resort palaces were built at the hotsprings of Lintong County, 18 miles (30 km) from Xi'an, close by the slopes of Black Horse Mountain. The First Emperor of Qin had a residence there, as did Han Wudi, the Martial Emperor. However, the strongest associations are with the Tang; Black Horse Mountain is still covered with the pine and cypress planted by Tang Xuanzong, and the present buildings have a Tang atmosphere.

Taizong commissioned his architect Yan Lide (Yen Li-te) to design a palace, the Tangquan, in 644. It became the favourite resort of Xuanzong, who spent every winter there from 745 to 755 in the company of Yang Guifei, the Imperial Concubine. The resort was much enlarged in 747 and renamed Huaqing Palace.

The complex was destroyed at the end of the Tang, and the present buildings, although many of them are named after Tang halls and pavilions, were built either at the end of the last century or during this.

The Baths The visitor to Huaqing Hotsprings may decide that perhaps the best way to get into the spirit of things is to take a bath. The water rises at a constant temperature of 109°F (43°C) and contains various minerals, including lime and manganese carbonate. The emperor's Nine Dragon Bath can be hired by four people for 40 minutes for 2 yuan. The Lotus and Crabapple Baths both take a couple for 40 minutes for 1 yuan, and there are other cheaper baths. The Huaqing Guesthouse (see page 19) also has its own baths. Total capacity at the springs is said to be over 400 people at a time.

The 'Imperial Concubine's Bath' is usually shown to tourists and so is not available for use. It is said to be on the site of the Hibiscus Bath, used by Yang Guifei. The present building is rather disappointing. The site of the real Tang baths, next to the 'Imperial Concubine's Bath', is now (1983) being excavated.

The Site of the Xi'an Incident The Five Chamber Building, just behind the 'Imperial Concubine's Bath', contains the bedroom used by Chiang Kai-shek on the eve of the Xi'an Incident of 12th December 1936. Chiang, pursuing his policy of appeasement, had been trying to suppress the Communists, instead of using his forces against the encroaching Japanese. His own troops at Xi'an, led by Zhang Xueliang, mutinied. Hearing gunfire, the Generalissimo ran halfway up Black Horse Mountain and hid behind a large rock. He was eventually found later in the day, minus one shoe and his false teeth, and arrested. Zhou Enlai participated in the negotiations which followed, and Chiang was released after pledging his support for a united front against the Japanese. The position of his hiding place is now marked by an iron chain. The Kiosk Commemorating the Capture of Chiang Kai-shek is a dignified Grecian structure with Doric columns. It was originally erected by the Nationalists to celebrate the escape of their leader and named the Pavilion of National Regeneration. (For the background to the Xi'an Incident see page 78).

Buddhism during and after the Golden Age
Background

During the Tang, Chang'an became the main centre of Buddhist learning in East Asia. The first contacts between adherents of Buddhism and the Chinese were probably made during the reign of the Martial Emperor, Han Wudi (140 – 86 BC) as a result of the opening of the Silk Road. During the following centuries this central Asian route, with Chang'an as its eastern terminus, remained the principal one by which Buddhism reached China. Today a number of monuments bear witness to the importance of Buddhism in the city's history. Most famous are two prominent landmarks, the Big and the Little Goose Pagodas (see pages 67 and 71). Also in reasonable condition is Da Cien Temple (of which the Big Goose Pagoda is a part), and two interesting temples south of the city, the Xingjiao and the Xiangji Temples (see pages 70 and 72). Some other Buddhist temples have survived in various states of disrepair but may prove worth visiting, as much for the setting and the journey there as for the temple buildings themselves.

Several of the surviving temples and pagodas have particular associations with Buddhist monks, scholars and translators who made the journey from Chang'an to India in search of enlightenment, the Buddhist scriptures and, possibly, adventure. Some 200 Chinese monks are recorded as travelling from Chang'an to India between the third and the eighth centuries. Conversely, a number of central Asian and Indian monks came to Chang'an, but they are less well documented than the Chinese travellers.

Best known of these monks is Xuanzhuang (Hsuan-chuang or Hsuan-tsang) who is today the most popular figure in the whole history of Chinese Buddhism. The Tang monk, as he is often simply called, is the hero of the long 16th-century Chinese novel *Monkey*, or sometimes known as *Journey to the West*, which is very loosely based on Xuanzhuang's travels. A scholar and translator, Xuanzhuang's 17-year journey took him to Nālandā (near Patna), then the greatest centre of Buddhist learning in India.

On his return he became abbot of Da Cien Temple (see page 68) where he spent the rest of his life working on translations of Buddhist texts that he had brought from India. His remains were interred under a pagoda which is part of Xingjiao Temple, or the Temple of Flourishing Teaching (see page 70).

By the early eighth century, Chang'an had a total of 64 monasteries and 27 nunneries. Much of the scholarship that resulted in the development of two important Buddhist sects — Pure Land and True Word — was done in the city. But the monasteries fulfilled a number of different roles, not only translating, studying and propagating religion, but also patronizing the arts, providing accommodation and even some banking facilties. They grew extremely rich, and Buddhism began to enjoy immense popularity at every level of society. The Tang emperors, however, were ambivalent in their support of the foreign religion. They claimed that Laozi (Lao-tzu), the founder of China's indigenous religion Daoism (Taoism), was their ancestor. Increasingly the success of the great temple-monasteries provoked resistance, and attempts were made to limit their power and wealth. Finally in 841 the insane Daoist Emperor Tang Wuzong ordered the dissolution of the monasteries and the return of the monks and nuns to secular life. There followed a period of four years of Buddhist persecution when almost all the temple-monasteries were destroyed. Though many of them were refounded after 845, and some of them survive to this day, Buddhism never completely recovered in China. And, after the destruction of Chang'an at the end of the Tang, the city lost its position as a centre of Buddhist learning for good.

Sights

Daxingshan Temple

Daxingshan Temple was the greatest Buddhist establishment of the Sui and Tang, but since the tenth century it has been destroyed and rebuilt several times, the latest reconstruction being in 1956. Today its grounds have been turned into a rather ordinary park (Xinfeng Park) and, although the main buildings have been repainted, the main courtyard is locked. Further restoration is planned.

The temple is said to date back to the third century when it was known as the Zunshan Temple. It was refounded during the Sui when it was given its present name, and became the headquarters of an order with a network of 45 prefectural temples, all established by the founder of the Sui Dynasty, Yang Jian. It became a great centre of Buddhist art and learning during the Tang, and the Tang monk, Xuanzhuang, hero of the famous Chinese novel *Monkey*, stayed there during the seventh century. Most of the buildings were destroyed during the great Buddhist persecution of 841 – 5, and whatever survived disappeared at the end of the Tang. The temple was rebuilt under the Ming and again restored in 1785 by an expert on Tang Dynasty Chang'an called Bi Yuan (1730 – 97). After its reconstruction in 1956 it was used by a community of lamaist monks until the Cultural Revolution (1966 – 76). Today it houses the Xi'an Buddhist Association.

To get there by public transport take bus 3 to the stop nearest the Big Goose Pagoda and then walk along Chang'an Lu until you come to a large market. Xinfeng Park, where the temple is situated, is down a narrow street just beyond.

The Temple of the Recumbent Dragon

The Temple of the Recumbent Dragon (Wolongsi), believed to be of Sui foundation, suffered particularly badly during the Cultural Revolution (1966 – 76). Virtually all the artwork is gone, and only a few portions of one hall remain. It now houses a factory. Should you wish to go there turn left at the entrance of the Shaanxi Museum and walk north along Baishulin Jie. The factory is down a dirt path between nos 25 and 27.

Huayan Temple

Huayan Temple was founded by the first patriarch of the Huayan sect of Buddhism, the monk Dushun (Tu-shun, 557 – 640), during the reign of Tang Taizong. It is located in the Fanchuan area 12 miles (20 km) south of Xi'an, and was one of the original Eight Great Temples of Fanchuan which flourished during the Tang. Two pagodas have survived from the Tang, indeed the only structures to have withstood an earthquake during the Qing Dynasty. One of the brick pagodas is 75 feet (23 m) high, and is square, like the Big Goose Pagoda, with seven storeys; the other is smaller with four storeys, hexagonal in form.

Caotang Temple

Sometimes translated as the Straw Hut Temple, Caotang Temple was founded during the Tang. Surrounded by fields, it lies south of the town of Huxian about 35 miles (55 km) southwest of Xi'an. Transportation is difficult and the temple has not been commonly visited. Restoration work was under way in 1982.

The temple was built on the site of a palace where Kumārajīva, a fourth-century translator of Buddhist scriptures, once worked and taught. Kumārajīva's translations, known for their elegant style rather than for their accuracy, have been used continuously down to modern times. The ashes of Kumārajīva are beneath a stone stupa, thought to be Tang, about 6½ feet (2 m) high, inside a small pavilion. In front there are some old cypress trees and a well. Other temple buildings include bell and tablet pavilions and a main hall.

The Big Goose Pagoda and Da Cien Temple

The Big Goose Pagoda, perhaps the most beautiful building left in Xi'an today, is one of the city's most outstanding landmarks. The adjacent Da Cien Temple is the city's best-preserved Buddhist temple complex.

Situated 2½ miles (4 km) south of the walled city at the end of Yanta Lu, or Goose Pagoda Road, the temple and pagoda are on the site of an earlier

Sui temple. Da Cien Temple was established in 647 by Li Zhi, who became Emperor Tang Gaozong in 649, in memory of his mother Empress Wende.

The Big Goose Pagoda The pagoda was completed in 652, and was built at the request of the famous Tang monk, Xuanzhuang, whose pilgrimage to India is immortalized in the 16th-century Chinese novel *Monkey*, or *Journey to the West*. Xuanzhuang asked the Emperor Gaozong to build a large stone stupa of a kind he had seen on his travels. The emperor offered a compromise brick structure of five storeys, about 175 feet (53 m) high, which was completed in 652. This was originally called the Scripture Pagoda and according to tradition it housed the collection of sūtras that Xuanzhuang had brought back from India, although this is now questioned. It is now called the Big Goose Pagoda although the reason for the name has never been satisfactorily explained.

Sometime between 701 and 704, at the end of the reign of Empress Wu, five more storeys were added to the pagoda, giving it a sharper, more pointed form than it has today. It was later damaged, probably by fire, and reduced to the seven storeys to be seen today. It is a simple, powerful, harmonious structure, but ironically, not the form that it was intended to be.

The Big Goose Pagoda rises 210 feet (64 m) to the north of the other temple buildings, and is the only remaining Tang building in the complex. On the pedestal, at the entrance to the first storey, are a number of Tang inscriptions and engravings set into the base of the pagoda. At the southern entrance are copies of prefaces to the translations of Xuanzhuang by the Emperors Taizong and Gaozong in the calligraphy of Chu Suiliang (Ch'u Sui-liang). Over the lintel of the western entrance is an engraving of Śākyamuni and other Buddhist figures in an elegant hall in Tang architectural style. Other tablets, inscribed during the Ming (1368–1644) recount the exploits of the Tang monk. It is possible to climb up inside the internal wooden staircase to the top of the pagoda, which commands a fine panoramic view.

Da Cien Temple During the Tang Da Cien Temple was a considerable establishment. No fewer than 1897 rooms were distributed around 13 courtyards, and there were about 300 resident monks. It contained paintings by the leading artists of the day, and had the finest peony garden in the capital.

Although the temple was one of four to continue functioning after the great Buddhist persecution of 841–5, it was destroyed at the end of the Tang (907). Since then it has been ruined and restored several times, but on a diminished scale. The last major restoration was in 1954, when the pedestal of the pagoda was widened.

The temple entrance is on the south side. Outside is a stone lamp given by the Japanese city of Kyōto. Within are the Bell and Drum Towers, to the right and left respectively, and a path leading to the Great Hall. This

contains three statues of Buddhas, surrounded by 18 clay figures of Śākyamuni Buddha's disciples (the disciples are known as *arhat* in Sanskrit, *luohan* in Chinese). It is claimed that both the building and the statues inside were made in 1466. To the east of the Great Hall are several small stone pagodas marking the remains of monks of the Qing period (1644 – 1911).

If you want to go there by public transport, take bus 5 from the railway station. The temple buildings are usually locked. Ask to be let in by the custodian, who also sells tickets to climb the pagoda.

Xingjiao Temple

This interesting temple is in a fine setting, overlooking the Fanchuan River, 14 miles (22 km) southeast of Xi'an, just beyond the village of Duqu. One of the Eight Great Temples of Fanchuan, Xingjiao Temple, or the Temple of Flourishing Teaching, was built in 669 by Tang Gaozong as a memorial to the Tang monk Xuanzhuang (see page 65), together with a tall brick pagoda covering his ashes. The temple was restored in 828, though by 839 it again lay abandoned according to an inscription on Xuanzhuang's pagoda. In one form or another the temple survived down to the 19th century when all the buildings were destroyed except the main pagoda and two smaller ones belonging to two of Xuanzhuang's disciples. The temple was again rebuilt, partly in 1922, partly in 1939. Five monks were living there in 1981, and the abbot was a member of the Conference of Chinese Buddhists.

The three pagodas stand to the west, in the Cien Pagoda Courtyard, a walled enclosure. The tall central one is dedicated to Xuanzhuang. It is a beautiful five-storey brick structure, imitating one of wood with brackets in relief. On stylistic grounds there is some doubt whether the present erection may date from the ninth century rather than the seventh. A small pavilion next to the pagoda has a modern copy of a stone engraving of Xuanzhuang, carrying the scriptures in what might be described as a sūtra-backpack.

On either side of the principal pagoda are those of Xuanzhuang's two translation assistants. Each is of three storeys. On the west side is that of Kuijī (K'uei-chi, 632 – 682), nephew of General Yuchi Jingde (a general of Emperor Tang Taizong). It was erected during the Tang. On the other side is the pagoda of Yuance (Yüan-ts'e), a Korean follower of Xuanzhuang. This was built later, in 1115.

At the entrance to the complex are the Bell and Drum Towers, 20th century but retaining their original instruments of the 19th century or earlier. Facing the entrance is the Great Hall of the Buddha, built in 1939, which contains a bronze, Ming-period Buddha. The Preaching Hall behind was built in 1922 and contains a number of statues including a bronze Amitābha Buddha, Ming-period, and a Śākyamuni Buddha of the same date as the hall.

In the Eastern Courtyard is the two-storey Library, built in 1922 and restored in 1939. It contains a white jade Buddha from Burma. The library proper is on the upper floor. The temple possesses some Tang Dynasty sūtras, written in Sanskrit, and formerly owned some Song editions of Chinese Buddhist works, though these are now in the Shaanxi Library in Xi'an. The temple has collections of the great Tang translations of Xuanzhuang and others, in 20th-century editions.

To get there by public transport take one of the infrequent country buses that run between the South Gate and the temple.

The Little Goose Pagoda and Da Jianfu Temple

The Little Goose Pagoda is one of Xi'an's major landmarks. Situated less than a mile south of the walled city, the 13-storey eighth-century pagoda is all that remains of the once flourishing Da Jianfu Temple. The temple, established in 684 in honour of Emperor Gaozong, was particularly associated with the pilgrim Yijing (I-ching), who settled there in the early eighth century to translate texts he had brought back with him from India. Although the temple continued to function after the Buddhist persecutions of 841 – 3, everything was destroyed save the Littre Goose Pagoda, together with an old locust tree said to have been planted during the Tang. Later, more modest temple buildings were erected next to the pagoda.

The pagoda has not survived completely unscathed. When it was completed in 707 the brick structure had 15 storeys, but it was damaged during a series of earthquakes in the late 15th and 16th centuries. The pagoda was split from top to bottom by the impact of an earthquake measuring 6¼ on the Richter scale in 1487, but it did not fall. In 1556 another quake, 8 on the Richter scale, had its epicentre near Huaxian, 47 miles (75 km) east of Xi'an. This one had the effect of throwing the two sides of the pagoda together again, but also dislodging the top two storeys.

The Little Goose Pagoda has remained to this day with only 13 storeys, 141 feet (43 m) high. Expert opinion is divided about the original appearance of the building (models of different designs are on display at the temple), and this is one reason that a complete restoration has never been attempted. A new internal staircase was put up in 1965 and it is possible to climb right to the top and look out over the fields to the walled city to the north.

At the base of the pagoda there are some Tang-period engravings of bodhisattvas on the stone lintels. There is also a tablet commemorating a restoration of the pagoda in 1116 and another engraved during the Qing (1644 – 1911) with information about the earthquakes. A stone tablet dated 1692 gives some idea of what the temple and pagoda would have looked like at that date, except that the pagoda is represented with 15 storeys. Standing in one of the courtyards is a large bell, dated 1192, originally from Wugong County, west of Xi'an, and moved to the temple about five centuries later. Above the room used for official briefings is an exhibition room with Buddhist statues from the Tang and later dynasties, Buddhist scriptures including some genuine Song and Ming editions, and a series of drawings and photographs of the Little Goose Pagoda.

Xiangji Temple

Xiangji Temple, which has an 11-storey pagoda built in 706, lies due south of Xi'an, some 12 miles (20 km) away, close to the town of Wangqu. The square brick pagoda was built over the ashes of the Buddhist monk Shandao, one of the patriarchs of Pure Land Buddhism which preached salvation through faith rather than meditation. It was built by a disciple named Jingye, who is himself commemorated by a smaller five-storey brick pagoda nearby. The pagoda of Shandao is similar in some respects to that of Xuanzhuang at the Temple of Flourishing Teaching, and imitates a wooden structure and has brackets in relief. Around the pagodas were originally the buildings of one of the great temple-monasteries of Tang Chang'an, although these have long since disappeared.

On the occasion of the 1300th anniversary of Shandao's death in 681, which fell, by Chinese reckoning, on 14th May 1980, a major restoration of the temple was completed. The Great Hall of the Buddha was rebuilt, and a Japanese Buddhist delegation presented a figure of the monk Shandao. It is now on view inside the hall together with a figure of Amitābha Buddha which was brought from a Peking museum.

It is difficult to reach the temple by public transport and the journey may take over two hours. Bus 15 leaves you at a village four miles from the temple, and from there you have to take a second bus which runs irregularly, or walk. However, the surrounding countryside of extensive upland wheatfields and the pagodas themselves are worth visiting if you have the time.

Period Five: Medieval and Modern Xi'an 907 to 1949

Background

With the destruction of Chang'an at the end of the Tang, the city lost its political splendour and power for good. Thereafter it remained a regional centre, for the most part out of the mainstream of political developments. The real economic centre of China had already moved away from Chang'an, further to the southeast, during the late Tang. After 907 the Xi'an area became progressively more impoverished and culturally backward. Much of the history in the following millenium is a dismal repetitious account of droughts and floods, famines and peasant insurrections.

Daoism continued to find adherents, and remnants of Daoist temples (see pages 79—82) can be seen in Xi'an today, despite the destruction of the Cultural Revolution. Islam, which had first been introduced into Chang'an by Arab merchants during the Tang, also flourished. Xi'an's beautiful Great Mosque is still functioning and can be visited by foreign visitors (see page 78).

Between the fall of the Tang and the establishment of the Ming Dynasty in 1369, the city changed its name many times. But in 1369 the city was renamed Xi'an Fu, the Prefecture of Western Peace. It was to remain as Xi'an from then on, except for the last year of the Ming Dynasty (1644), when the peasant leader Li Zicheng captured the city and renamed it Chang'an. (The name Chang'an survives today as the name of the county town immediately south of Xi'an.)

Ming Dynasty In 1370 Zhu Yuanzhang, the first emperor of the Ming Dynasty, gave Xi'an to his second son, Zhu Shuang, as fief. Zhu Shuang became Prince of Qin, using the old name for the area. A palace was constructed for him and the city substantially rebuilt on the site of the Imperial City section of the Tang capital, covering approximately one-sixth of the area of the former city. The prince did not take up residence until 1378, when the palace and the walls and gates of the city had already been completed. The palace, which was in the northeast part of the city, no longer exists but much of 14th-century Xi'an still survives, notably the Bell and Drum Towers and the city wall and gates (see pages 83 and 82).

Qing Dynasty When the Manchus established the last imperial dynasty of China, the Qing, in 1646, Xi'an was garrisoned by Manchu troops. They occupied the northeast section of the city, which was walled off. These soldiers were referred to, inaccurately, as 'Tartars' in European accounts.

During the 18th century the city, or at least its officials and merchants, enjoyed some prosperity, as indicated by the great development of *Qinqiang* opera during this time (see page 30). However, the 19th century was less happy with natural calamities following fast behind a disastrous Muslim rebellion (1862 – 1873).

In 1900 Xi'an again became a capital of sorts during the Boxer War when the Empress Dowager Cixi (Tz'u-hsi), with her captive emperor, the powerless Guangxu (Kuang-hsu), fled in disguise from Peking. They stayed for over a year in Xi'an, beyond the reach of the western powers, while peace was being negotiated.

In 1911 when a nationwide revolution overthrew the Qing regime, resistance by the garrison in Xi'an collapsed without much of a struggle. But a terrible massacre of the Manchus ensued. Between 10,000 and 20,000 died, including a few unlucky foreigners, and most of the buildings in the Manchu quarter were burnt down. Such bloodletting and destruction did not occur in other cities. Much of the killing in Xi'an was evidently done by the Muslims, in revenge for the suppression of their rebellion 40 years earlier.

Xi'an in the Republican Era During the Republican era of 1911 to 1949 Xi'an gradually became less isolated from the outer world. Before the revolution the city had already established its first telegraph office (in 1885) and international post office (in 1902). The railway did not reach Xi'an until 1934 but westerners started to visit the city in increasing numbers from the turn of the century onwards, usually making contact with the China Inland Mission, the Scandinavian Alliance Mission or the English Baptists, all of whom were represented in the city. They returned, often to write books, informing (and more often, misinforming) the outside world about 'ancient Sian-fu'.

It will be long before the City of Western Peace becomes the resort of sightseers. Yet Sian and its neighbourhood provide more sights to see than most inland Chinese capitals, in case the blessed day of trains de luxe and steam-heated hotels should ever dawn for it. The rolling plain, all round as far as you can see, is full of mounds and barrows; and two noble pagodas invite inspection. Or you can mount the wall and study the whole flat extent of the city; you can ascend the Drum Tower, and from the vast darkness of its loft look out towards the turquoise roofs of the Mahometan mosque, and, beyond these, to the orange gables of the Imperial Palace, where the Grand Dowager pitched her flying tents in 1900.

(From *On the Eaves of the World* by Reginald Farrar 1917)

Xi'an was of some strategic importance during the struggle for power in the 1920s and '30s. When in 1926, it was occupied by a pro-Nationalist Shaanxi general, Yang Hucheng, the city was promptly surrounded by an anti-Nationalist force. So began the six-month Siege of Xi'an. When it was finally lifted, some 50,000 were said to have died. Revolution Park marks the place where they were buried (see page 84).

In the struggle between Communist and Nationalist forces, Xi'an came to the forefront in 1936, when Huaqing Hotsprings was the scene of the

so-called Xi'an Incident (see page 63). Chiang Kai-Shek, intent on getting rid of domestic Communist opposition before putting up resistance to the invading Japanese, was arrested by two Nationalist generals, Yang Hucheng and the leader of the displaced Northeastern Army, Zhang Xueliang, and forced to agree to join the Communists against the common enemy, the Japanese. Xi'an then became a vital link between the Communist headquarters in Yan'an and the outside world through the establishment of Eighth Route Army Office (see page 84).

During the Anti-Japanese War, Xi'an was bombed, but never occupied, by the Japanese. After the end of the war, the city was controlled by Nationalist troops until it was taken by Communist forces on 20th May 1949. The People's Republic of China was inaugurated less than five months later.

Sights

The Great Mosque

This beautiful mosque lies close by the Drum Tower in Huajue Xiang surrounded by the old houses and narrow lanes of Xi'an's Muslim, or *Hui*, community. The mosque is still active: on ordinary days about 500 men pray there, with perhaps 2000 on Fridays. Of the three or four functioning mosques in the city this is the only one which is open to visitors although non-Muslims would not be admitted at prayer times.

Islam has been the most enduring of all faiths in Xi'an. It was first introduced by Arab merchants during the Tang Dynasty, and flourished during the Yuan (1279 —1368). The Muslims gradually became concentrated on the northwestern part of the walled city, where they remain to this day. The community now numbers roughly 30,000. There were said to be 14 mosques open before the Cultural Revolution put a stop to Muslim privileges. But today, the community is regaining its lost ground. It has its own graveyard, primary school, slaughterhouse, foodshops and restaurants (these are popular with the Han Chinese as well). Although the Muslims generally work on Fridays, they do observe Ramadan, the month of fasting.

The Great Mosque survived the Cultural Revolution virtually unscathed and remains an outstanding Chinese re-interpretation of an Islamic place of worship. It was founded in 742, according to a stone tablet in the mosque, but nothing from the Tang survives. The present layout dates from the 14th century and restoration work was done in 1527, 1606 and 1768. The mosque occupies a rectangle 820 feet by 155 feet (250 m by 47 m), divided into four courtyards. Throughout there are walls with decoratively carved brick reliefs and the buildings are roofed with turquoise tiles.

The **first courtyard,** which was restored in 1981, has an elaborate wooden arch 29½ feet (9 m) high dating from the 17th century. Most visitors enter the mosque through a gate leading into the **second courtyard.** This contains a stone arch and two free-standing steles. One bears the calligraphy of a famous Song master Mi Fu (1051 — 1107), the other has that of Dong Qichang of the Ming.

At the entrance to the **third courtyard** is a Stele Hall with tablets of the Ming and Qing periods inscribed in Chinese, Arabic and Persian. The Stele of the Months, written in Arabic by an imam in 1733, contains information about the Islamic calendar.

In the middle of the third courtyard is the minaret, an octagonal pagoda with a triple roof of turquoise tiles, known as the Shengxin Tower. On either side are sets of rooms. In one section, next to the imams' living quarters, there is a Qing Dynasty map of the Islamic world painted by Chinese Muslims. In the centre is the black cube of the Kaaba at Mecca with representations of Medina, Syria, Egypt, Yemen, Iraq, Bukhara, Khorassan, Samarkand, India, the Sudan and other places. In the same room is kept an illuminated Qur'ān handwritten during the Qing Dynasty.

The **fourth courtyard,** the principal one of the complex, contains the Prayer Hall. By the entrance is a small room with an upright stele recording in Chinese the foundation of the mosque in 742. The stone itself is not thought to be original. In front of the entrance is the ornamental **Phoenix Pavilion** with a board proclaiming the 'One Truth' of the One God, written during the Ming. Behind the Phoenix Pavilion are two fountains flanked by two small stele pavilions and then behind is the broad, raised stone terrace used for worship.

The large **Prayer Hall** dates from the Ming; the board outside the main door was bestowed by the Yongle Emperor (reigned 1403 — 1424). The ornate woodwork inside is mainly of this period. There is a coffered ceiling, each panel containing different Arabic inscriptions. The mihrab at the far end has some fine carving, and retains some original carving.

To walk to the Great Mosque go north along the street that passes under the Drum Tower, and take the first left. A sign in English indicates the way.

The Temple of the Eight Immortals

China's indigenous religion, Daoism (Taoism) is best represented in Xi'an by the Temple of the Eight Immortals (Ba Xian An).

Located just east of the city wall, it housed 100 monks as recently as 20 years ago. But at the start of the Cultural Revolution in 1966 half the buildings were demolished, and those that remained were converted into a machine plant. Today, however, one of the halls has been recently restored, and the temple is now functioning again in a small way.

Although no foundation stele exists, it is thought the temple was established during the Northern Song (960 —1127). It expanded during the

Yuan and Ming, and became particularly important during the Qing. When the imperial court was in exile in Xi'an (1900 – 01), the Empress Dowager Cixi (Tz'u-hsi, 1835 – 1908) grew especially fond of the temple and used to go there to paint peonies.

Take trolleybus 5 one stop beyond the wall, walk back along Changle Lu and take the first left. When that road ends, bear right and then left. The temple compound is on the right, hidden behind high walls, but one small gate should be open.

Eastern Peak Temple

This Daoist complex, founded in 1116, is situated about 50 yards from the northwest corner of the East Gate, and is now a primary school. The temple was dedicated to the cult of Tai Shan, the most important of the sacred mountains of China. Today, while all the altars have of course gone, there are just a few traces of the once-famous frescoes. A small Qing pavilion at the rear of the compound, in bad condition, has additional murals.

The Temple of the Town God

Within walking distance of the Bell Tower, this temple is now a school and warehouse but some of the buildings are still in reasonable condition. A walk to the temple from Xi Dajie (West Avenue) will take you to the interesting old Muslim quarter. The temple dates back to 1389, but was moved to its present site in 1432. It has been rebuilt and restored many times, notably in 1723 when materials were utilized from the 14th-century palace of the Prince of Qin, Zhu Shuang. The main hall, built in 1723, survives with richly carved doors and a bright blue-tiled roof.

To get there walk along Xi Dajie to number 257, then take the small lane running north through the Muslim quarter, past an active mosque on the left. Turn right at the T-intersection, then right again, down a cobbled alley. At the end of this lane turn right again into the temple gates.

The Ming City Wall and Gates

Xi'an's 14th-century city wall still stands, although today it is intersected by a few modern roads to ease transport in and out of the city. It is one of the best examples of a Ming city wall that has survived. The circumference is 7.4 miles (11.9 km), and it is 40 feet (12 m) high, 40 – 46 feet (12 – 14 m) wide at the top and 49 – 59 feet (15 – 18 m) wide at the bottom. It is surrounded by a moat, now virtually dried up.

The Ming city gates face the four cardinal points, set off-centre in each of the sides of the rectangular wall. Originally each gate had two structures.

On the city wall itself was the gate tower, a triple-eaved building 114 feet (34.6 m) long, and beyond was the massive, single-roofed archers' tower, 175 feet (53.2 m) in length, with 48 openings on the outer face from which missiles could be fired on a potential enemy. Today the East and West Gates survive intact. The West Gate is in the better condition of the two. It was restored in 1962 and contains a small museum. Of the North Gate only the outer archers' tower remains, and the south gate, last restored in 1958, only retains the gate tower. There are, however, plans for further restoration.

The Bell Tower

Each Ming city had a bell tower and a drum tower. The bell was sounded at dawn and the drum at dusk. The two buildings still exist in many Chinese cities, but those at Xi'an are the best known in China.

The Bell Tower was built in 1384 at the intersection of Xi Dajie (West Avenue) and Guangji Jie. This was the centre of the site of the old Tang Imperial City, where the Tang government offices had been located. The tower was removed in 1582 and rebuilt in its present position in the centre of the southern section of the walled city, overlooking the four avenues which lead to the four gates. It was restored in 1739. Now seemingly enmeshed in trolleybus overhead wires, it is nevertheless proudly regarded as the symbol of the city.

The Bell Tower is set on a square brick platform, each side of which is 116 feet (35.5 m) long, with an arched gateway at ground level. The platform is 28 feet (8.6 m) high and on top of it is a triple-eaved, two-storeyed wooden structure, a further 90 feet (27.4 m) high. There is a fine view in all directions from the parapet on the second floor. The inside is remarkable as an example of the very intricate roof truss system used in Ming and Qing Dynasty wooden architecture. The original great bell no longer exists, but a small Ming-period bell is kept on a corner of the brick platform.

The Drum Tower

The Drum Tower, in contrast to the nearby Bell Tower, is rectangular, though in other respects it is very similar in style. It was first built in 1380, and restored in 1669, 1739 and 1953. The brick base, on which the wooden structure is built, is 172 feet (52.6 m) long, 125 feet (38 m) wide, and 25 feet (7.7 m) high. The road goes straight through it, under a vaulted archway. The triple-roofed, two-storeyed wooden building is a further 83 feet (25.3 m) high off its brick platform. The second storey, which is surrounded by a parapet, is now used as an antique shop. The immediate surroundings are more interesting than those of the Bell Tower. Less encumbered by wires, the Drum Tower looks down on the irregular grey-tiled roofs of the Muslim quarter.

Revolution Park

The park, in the northeast of the walled city, marks the place where those who died in the 1926 Siege of Xi'an are buried. Anti-nationalist forces laid siege to Xi'an on 15th May 1926 after the city had been occupied by a pro-Nationalist general Yang Hucheng. The city held out despite appalling starvation and in the face of a bombing attack, until 28th November 1926, when the siege was finally lifted. Yang Hucheng wrote the funeral couplet for those 50,000 inhabitants and refugees who are said to have died during the siege:

> They led glorious lives and died a glorious death.
> Their merits are known throughout Shaanxi, as are their regrets.

The park contains a three-storeyed pagoda erected in 1927.

The Eighth Route Army Office Museum

Near Revolution Park at 1, Qixianzhuang, just off Beixin Jie, is the Eighth Route Army Office, which is now a museum. It was founded immediately after the Xi'an Incident which had resulted in the Nationalists and Communists joining forces against the Japanese (see page 78). Initially called the Red Army Liaison Office, the name was changed in September 1937.

The office linked the headquarters of the Communist Party in Yan'an in northern Shaanxi with the outside world in the struggle against the Japanese. It obtained vital supplies for Yan'an, helped recruits make their way there, and publicized the policies of the party leadership. The office remained functioning until July 1946. It is now preserved as it was during the Anti-Japanese War.

The Office occupies a series of plain, but attractive grey and white one-storey buildings set around four courtyards. There is an exhibition room with many photographs taken in Shaanxi during the 1930s and '40s. Visitors are also shown the rooms where important Communist leaders stayed. These included Zhou Enlai, Zhu De, Peng Dehuai, Ye Jianying and Deng Xiaoping. The Canadian doctor Norman Bethune, later to become almost a cult figure in China, was also there.

The office still has its 1939 Chevrolet, originally imported from Hong Kong and used for urgent missions to Yan'an. The radio room contains the old transmitter and receiver. Since 1964 the director of the museum has been a veteran solider, Tang Bin. He joined the Communist Fourth Route Army in Sichuan in 1933, when he was only 16, and eventually became a guard at the Eighth Route Army Office in Lanzhou from 1938 to 1946, later rising to be a company commander in the air force.

Period Six: Xi'an under the People's Republic

Background

Xi'an has grown physically much larger in the past 30 years, the population has increased and new industries, textiles in particular, have been established. The initial impetus for this growth came from the government whose policy was to give priority to the development of cities of the interior. In 1949 the city did not extend much further than the walled city, covering only 5 square miles (13.2 sq km). Today the city has spread out to cover some 38½ square miles (100 sq km), an area even larger than the Tang capital of Chang'an which had an area of 31.2 square miles (81 sq km), within the outer walls. The modern city is not so regular in its layout as its great predecessor, and it extends further to the east and west than the Tang city.

The population has increased rapidly since the 1930s when it was between 200,000 and 300,000. Today it is 2.8 million according to the most recent published figure. This includes the people living in seven urban districts, one county (Chang'an) and 70 communes. The urban population is probably around 1.6 million.

Visitors to Xi'an may see something of the city's recent industrial and social development through visits to model factories, hospitals, schools, district neighbourhoods, and communes.

Another place of major interest to foreign visitors is the Shaanxi Museum. Although developed earlier, it was formally established in 1952. This is the principal museum of Shaanxi Province and is one of the best of its kind in China (see page 87).

Sights

Factories

Industry barely existed in Xi'an in the early 1930s. No serious development was practicable before the opening of the Longhai Railway in 1934. By 1949 the city only had a few flour mills, one cotton mill, a match factory and a small power plant. In the early 1950s industries were rapidly established to utilize the labour of the large numbers of people who had by then moved in from outlying areas. The city has only one minor steelworks; development has focused on textiles and a range of light manufacturing industries.

New industrial districts have now grown up to the east and west of the old city. At **Bailuyuan,** due east of the walled city (where the neolithic settlement of Banpo was discovered), there is now a large textile producing satellite town. Of the eight or so cotton mills in Xi'an, four of them, large state enterprises, are at Bailuyuan. In addition Bailuyuan has two printing and dyeing complexes, two dyeing and weaving factories, two small silk factories and a velveteen mill. The nearby town of Xianyang is also a textile centre.

On the western side of the city there are about a dozen factories manufacturing equipment for the generating and transmission of electricity. Most of these are on or near Daqing Lu. The **Xi'an High Voltage Electrical Insulator Works** is sometimes shown to interested visitors. Among the city's light industrial enterprises, the **Red Flag Watch Factory** at Weiqu has received visiting groups.

Schools and Universities

Xi'an already has a host of educational and research organizations. All children in the urban areas attend school up to senior middle school level. In the whole municipality there are more than 1000 primary schools and 258 middle schools (18 of which offer some form of specialized training). Of the two-dozen or so tertiary educational institutions for Shaanxi Province, the leading one of these is **Xi'an Jiaotong (Communications) University,** devoted to science and technology, located opposite Xingqing Park.

The **Xi'an Foreign Languages Institute, Shaanxi Normal University** (where teachers are trained) and **Northwestern University** (with a prominent archaeology department), are three other important establishments. Xi'an also contains a grand total of 80 scientific research institutes although whether all are actively involved in research is open to question.

Hospitals and Clinics

A greatly increased number of hospital beds are now available for the people of Xi'an, 12,000 in 1981 or one for every 233 inhabitants. The municipality has 60 odd hospitals, 26 factory clinics and 450 small clinics. Within the urban area proper there are 15 main hospitals, including a children's hospital, an infectious diseases hospital, a tuberculosis hospital and one psychiatric institution. Two of the hospitals are attached to the **Xi'an Medical College,** located in the southern part of the city. There are also six special health care centres and one psychiatric sanatorium in the city.

Neighbourhoods

Visitors are sometimes able to go to the subdistrict offices of the local government to see clinics, kindergartens and small-scale neighbourhood factories. The **Qingnian Road Neighbourhood** in the Lianhu District in particular has received foreigners.

Life in the residential districts of Xi'an has improved in a number of significant ways since 1949. In former days the city depended on well water, but this has now been largely replaced by tap water. Most of the city is now covered by a sewage system. In 1949 the city only had 17 buses. It now has a fairly comprehensive, if very overcrowded, public transport system of buses and trolleybuses. Roads have been surfaced and tree planting campaigns have improved the appearance of the streets.

Communes

Visitors are often taken to see the **Maqizhai People's Commune,** which occupies the area of the Tang Dynasty Daming Palace, just north of the Xi'an Railway Station, very close to the centre of the city. Interested parties can also go to the **Fenghuo People's Commune** of Liquan County although it is over 40 miles (60 km) from Xi'an in the direction of the Qian Ling. The Fenghuo Brigade (part of the commune) received a special certificate of merit from Premier Zhou Enlai (Chou En-lai) in December 1958, soon after the commune had been established.

Agriculture is important to the economy of Xi'an. The vast majority of the 1.2 million people in the Xi'an municipality who are employed outside the urban area, work in one of the municipality's 70 communes. The municipality controls 883 square miles (2295 sq km) of land area and much of this is cultivated. Principal cereals are winter wheat (sown in October, harvested in July) and maize (planted July, harvested September). The main cash crops are cotton (planted May, harvested between August and October) and rape seed. Fruit and vegetables are grown and sent into the city, particularly from the area on the fringe of the city.

Shaanxi Museum

The Shaanxi Museum, one of the finest museums in China, was formally established in 1952 and occupies the former Temple of Confucius. It is the principal museum for Shaanxi Province and displays artifacts brought from every part of the area. The 2600-odd exhibits are shown in chronological order to illustrate the history of Shaanxi — the usual organization of museums in China. Only the large stone sculptures are separate from this arrangement.

The Zhou, Qin, Han Gallery

In front of this first gallery is a fifth-century stone horse, from the north of the province. The gallery itself contains items dating from earliest times down to AD 220. There is a good collection of Zhou bronzes, pottery and jade. This includes a massive bronze *ding* tripod. Of the Warring States period there are various iron agricultural implements as well as a fine gold and silver inlaid bronze wine vessel, or *zun,* in the form of a rhinoceros

Shaanxi Museum

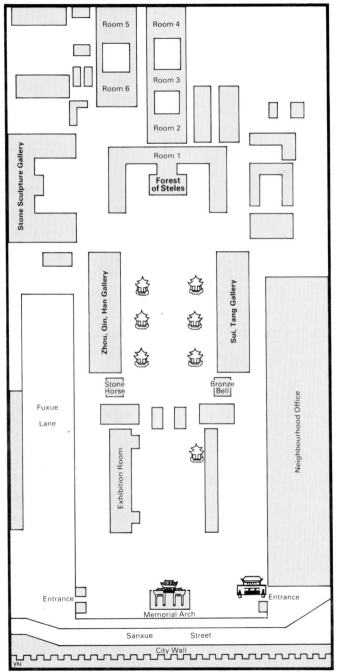

which was found near the tomb of Han Wudi, the Martial Emperor. From the Qin there are a number of objects discovered in and around the county town of Lintong, near the mausoleum of the First Emperor of Qin. There are Qin pottery figures, iron weights, coins and decorated building materials. The wide selection of Han Dynasty pieces include painted clay figurines, pottery models of buildings, weapons and decorated tiles and water pipes. There is a jade seal of an empress of the Western Han.

The Sui, Tang Gallery
Opposite the stone horse which is outside the first gallery there is an eighth-century Tang bronze bell. This is at the southern entrance of the Sui, Tang Gallery. But, if you want to view the exhibits chronologically, you should enter the gallery at the north entrance.

The Tang pottery on display is of the highest quality, much of it excavated in recent years. There are both painted and unpainted, glazed and unglazed examples. Of the polychrome pieces there is a superb pottery figure of a soldier in armour, discovered at Liquan and dated as 663. Of the tri-colour glazed statues one of the most interesting is a camel with a small orchestra on its carpeted back. There are also powerful figures of horses, and a number of representations of large-nosed, heavily-bearded central Asians.

Fine engraved Tang gold and silver vessels are in the gallery together with bronze mirrors and silver coins from Persia and Japan. Some copies of recently discovered tomb murals from the Qian Ling complex (see page 58) are on the walls.

The Stone Sculpture Gallery
This gallery, which is beside the Forest of Steles, has a collection of about 70 sculptures and relief carvings of unrivalled quality. However, not all of the stones are originals (in particular the horse from the tomb of Swift Cavalry General Huo Qubing is a reproduction). The most famous exhibits are the six bas-reliefs, four of them originals, from the Zhao Ling, the Mausoleum of Emperor Tang Taizong (see page 55). There are also a number of large animals which once lined the approaches to imperial tombs of the Han and Tang. At the end of the gallery are some Buddhist statues including a very beautiful torso of a bodhisattva, showing strong Indian influence, and an Avalokiteśvara on an elaborate lotus throne. Both are Tang period.

The Forest of Steles
This famous collection of over 1000 inscribed stones began in 1090 when a large Confucian collection of steles, cut in 837, was moved for safekeeping to the back of the Temple of Confucius. Thereafter the collection grew slowly and by the 18th century it had begun to be called by its present name, the Forest of Steles. It is the largest collection of its kind in China. This stone library is now a part of the Shaanxi Museum.

The art of making inscriptions on stone began in China at least as early as the fourth century BC. The earliest examples that have survived, which are of this date, are the ten Stone Drums of Qin. Recording a hunting party led by a Duke of Qin, they were discovered during the Tang Dynasty at Fengxiang, about 90 miles (145 km) west of Xi'an. The originals are now in Peking but a reproduction of one of them is on display in the Zhou, Qin, Han Gallery of the Shaanxi Museum.

From the Han Dynasty onwards flat stones were cut with either text or pictures in order to preserve the picture or text as well as to make it possible to reproduce them on paper by taking rubbings. These rubbings, made into either scrolls or books, have often served as models for calligraphy practice.

Accounts written by western visitors to Xi'an in the early part of this century indicate that they were much impressed by the aura of this famous collection of grey-black slabs of stone, even if few understood what they were. Today's foreign visitors may well feel the same, unless they have a competent guide-interpreter, since all explanatory notes for the collection are in Chinese.

As a rough guide, the contents of the Forest of Steles can be divided into four groups: works of literature and philosophy, historical records, calligraphy and pictorial stones. The pictorial stones, which may be of most immediate interest, are in Room Four together with some stones engraved with historical records. The pictorial stones are almost all relatively late, Ming or Qing (1368—1911). As well as landscapes and portraits — notably of Confucius and Bodhidarma — there are some interesting stones with allegorical pictures and some texts written to appear like pictures (it was a Qing fashion to create pictures composed of Chinese characters). In Room Three is the calligraphy collection which is of great importance, just as the art itself is much more developed and of greater significance than in the European world. There are two reconstructed examples of the calligraphy of Wang Xizhi (321-379) which have had immense influence on the art of the brush, together with pieces by many of the great Tang Dynasty masters.

For those who would like to see the famous Nestorian Stele, cut in 781, it is in Room Two, immediately to the left of the entrance. This records the history of the Nestorian Christian community at Chang'an from its founding in the seventh century by a Syrian missionary. Room One contains the nucleus of the collection, the set of 114 stones, engraved in 837 on both sides using a total of 650,252 characters with the definitive text of the Confucian Classics.

Recommended Reading

History and Religion

K Ch'en: *Buddhism in China, A Historical Survey* (Princeton University Press, Princeton, New Jersey, 1964)
J Bertram: *First Act in China: The Story of the Sian Mutiny* (1938, reprinted by Hyperion Press, Westport, Conn., 1973)
M Zanchen (Translated by Wang Zhao): *The Life of General Yang Hucheng* (Joint Publishing Company, Hong Kong, 1981)
E Reischauer: *Ennin's Diary* (Ronald Press Company, New York, 1955)
The Silk Road (20-part series published in *China Pictorial*, Beijing June 1979 to February 1981)

Arts and Archaeology

W Watson: *Ancient China, The Discoveries of Post-Liberation Archaeology* (BCC, London, 1974)
B Laufer: *Chinese Pottery of the Han Dynasty* (1909, reprinted by Charles E Tuttle, Vermont and Tokyo, 1962)

Literature

Y Inoue (Translated by J T Araki and E Seidensticker): *Lou-lan and Other Stories* (Kodansha International Limited, New York and San Francisco, 1979)
E R Hughes: *Two Chinese Poets, Vignettes of Han Life and Thought* (Princeton University Press, Princeton, New Jersey, 1960)
A Waley: *The Life and Times of Po Chu-i 772-846* (George Allen & Unwin, London, 1949)
J D Frodsham: *The Poems of Li Ho 791-817* (Oxford University Press, Oxford, 1970)

Early Twentieth-Century Travellers

Ernest Borst-Smith: *Caught in the Chinese Revolution: A Record of Risks and Rescue* (T Fisher Unwin, London, 1912)
Violet Cressy-Marcks: *Journey into China* (Hodder and Stoughton, London, 1940)
S Eliasson (Translated by K John): *Dragon Wang's River* (Methuen and Company Limited, London, 1957)
R Farrar: *On the Eaves of the World* (E Arnold, London, 1917)
P Fleming: *News From Tartary* (1936, reprinted by Futura Publications, London, 1980).
F H Nichols: *Through Hidden Shensi* (Charles Scribner's Sons, New York, 1902)
R Stirling Clark and A de C Sowerby: *Through Shen-Kan: The Account of the Clark Expedition in North China 1908-9* (T Fisher Unwin, London, 1912)

Useful Addresses

Airport, Xi'an City
Xiguan, tel. 41989
西安市民航站　西关

Antiques Store, Xi'an City
Drum Tower, tel. 28797
西安市文物商店　鼓楼

Arts and Crafts Store, Xi'an City
18 Nanxin Jie, tel. 28798
西安市工艺美术服务部　南新街18号

Bank of China, Shaanxi Branch
Jiefang Lu, tel. 26931
中国银行陕西分行　解放路

Bei Dajie Market
Bei Dajie (North Avenue) tel. 28305
北大街商场　北大街

Bureau of Foreign Trade, Shaanxi Province
Xincheng, tel. 22178
陕西省对外贸局　新城

Central Hospital, Xian City
Houzai Men, tel. 28916
西安市中心医院　后宰门

China International Travel Service (CITS), Xi'an Branch
Jiefang Lu, tel. 21191
中国国际旅行社西安分社　解放路

Civil Aviation Administration of China (CAAC)
296 Xishaomen (outside the West Gate), tel. 21855
中国民航　西梢门296号

Cloisonné Factory, Xi'an City
21 Yanta Lu
西安市金属工艺厂　雁塔路21号

Dong Dajie Department Store
Dong Dajie (East Avenue) tel. 25613
东大街百货商店　东大街

Exhibition Centre, Shaanxi Province
Longshoucun, Beijiao, tel. 61866
陕西省展览馆　北郊龙首村

Foreign Affairs Office, People's Government of Shaanxi Province
Visitors Reception Centre, Jianguo Lu, tel. 21363
陕西省人民政府外事办公室　信访室　建国路

Foreign Languages Bookstore, Shaanxi Province
Dong Dajie (East Avenue), tel. 22197
陕西省外文书店　东大街

Foreign Languages Institute, Xi'an
Wujiafen, Nanjiao, tel. 52956
西安外国语学院　南郊吴家坟

Friendship Store, Xi'an City
Nanxin Jie, tel. 21551
西安友谊商店　南新街

Friendship Taxi Company
Caochangpo, tel. 52281
西安友谊汽车公司　草场坡

Jade Carving Factory, Xi'an City
173 Xiyi Lu, tel. 22085
西安市玉石雕刻厂　西一路173号

Jiaotong University, Xi'an
26 Xianning Lu (opposite Xingqing Park), tel. 31231
西安交通大学　咸宁路26号

Jiefang Lu Department Store
Jiefang Lu, tel. 24348
解放路百货商店　解放路

Jiefang Market
Jiefang Shichang, tel. 28083
解放百货商场　解放市场

Library, Shaanxi Province
Xi Dajie (West Avenue), tel. 22420
陕西省图书馆　西大街

Long-distance Bus Stations:

Yuxiang Gate Bus Station
Huancheng Xi Lu, tel. 22061
玉祥门汽车站　环城西路

Jiefang Gate Bus Station
Huochezhan Guangchang Xi , tel. 24418
解放门汽车站　火车站广场西

Xiaonan Gate Bus Station
Huancheng Nan Lu, Western Section,
tel. 22563
小南门汽车站　环城南路

**Long-distance Telecommunications
Office, Xi'an City**
Bei Dajie (North Avenue), tel. 24007
西安长途电信局　北大街

Minsheng Department Store
Jiefang Lu, tel. 26651
民生百货商店　解放路

Northwestern University
65 Daxue Dong Lu, tel. 25036
西北工业大学　大学东路65号

Outer Districts Bus Station
Nanmen Wai, tel. 26695
远郊汽车站　南门外

Post Office, Xi'an City
Bei Dajie (North Avenue), tel. 25413
西安市邮政局　北大街

Railway Station, Xi'an
Huochezhan Guangchang, tel. 26976
西安火车站　火车站广场

**Special Arts and Crafts Factory,
Xi'an City**
Huancheng Xi Lu, tel. 28780
西安市特种工艺美术工厂　环城西路

Shaanxi Normal University
Wujiafen, Nanjiao, tel. 52946
陕西师范院　南郊吴家坟

Xin'an Market
Dong Dajie (East Avenue)
新安市场　东大街

Index of Places